ON THE EDGE OF PENTECOST

ON THE EDGE OF PENTECOST

A theological journey of transformation

TOM STUCKEY

Scripture quotations, unless stated otherwise, are from the
New Revised Standard Version of the Bible (Anglicized Edition)
© 1989, 1995 by the Division of Christian Education of the
National Council of the Churches of Christ in the United States
of America. Used by permission. All rights reserved.

ISBN 978-1-905958-12-2

First published by Inspire
4 John Wesley Road
Werrington
Peterborough PE4 6ZP

Typeset by Regent Typesetting, London
Printed and bound in Great Britain by
Athenaeum Press Ltd., Gateshead, Tyne & Wear

Dedicated to Ben and Sam

Contents

Acknowledgements

I told my wife eighteen months ago that I had no intention of writing another book. An explanation is therefore necessary. Our travels during the period of my Presidency of the Methodist Conference, the stories we heard, our journal record, my lectures, the articles in the *Methodist Recorder* and, above all, the people we met produced such a richness of resource that this book asked to be written. Thank you, Christine, for encouraging me to sit down and write it. Your comments on the many drafts have also helped to sharpen the detail and shape this final version.

I am again grateful to the Head of Publishing at Inspire, Natalie Watson. Given the relative success of my previous book, *Beyond the Box*, I could see a quick follow-up made sense but was unprepared for the enthusiastic way in which she seized upon my embryonic ideas, gave them a clear theological focus and introduced me to the concept of 'liminality'.

I also wish to thank members of my family, some of whom are named in the pages which follow. I was especially grateful when my daughter Joanne read some of the more sensitive sections of an earlier draft and gave me invaluable advice in the handling of intimate material.

Thanks are again offered to Eric Renouf who continues to do my proofreading, to Susan Hibbins of the Methodist Publishing House and Moira Sleight for permission to use parts of my articles which first appeared in the *Methodist Recorder*. In addition I am delighted to acknowledge the contribution and comments of Vernon White, Director of the Southern Theological Education and Training Scheme; Martyn Atkins, the current President of the Methodist Conference; Barbara Glasson for her poem (page 144) and Christopher Blake whose throw-away sentence (page 143) provoked me to write.

Finally, I record my thanks to innumerable friends and colleagues within the Methodist Church and beyond. In many ways you are co-writers of this book, for your stories have helped to shape mine.

Tom Stuckey
October 2007

Part 1

Crazy Ideas

1

Who Wants to be a Millionaire?

There is a hush of expectation. Four hundred representatives stand as the platform party take up their positions. Surrounding them in the galleries of the Riviera Centre, Torquay, are hundreds more: distinguished guests, bishops, leaders of Churches, representatives of local government, gaily dressed visitors from other parts of the world, rank-and-file members, the enthusiasts, the faithful and the curious. The date is Saturday 25 June 2005. This is the start of the Conference of the Methodist Church.

Each year Conference meets, as it has done since 1744, in different locations across Britain to deliberate and confer. The annual Conferences of the main political parties have replicated the Methodist format in their approach to business, though without the singing and praying.

Conference begins, as it has done for many years, with Charles Wesley's hymn, 'And are we yet alive?' The verses reflect the turbulent story of the Methodist people:

What troubles have we seen,
What conflicts have we passed,
Fightings without, and fears within,
Since we assembled last!

The verse before the final flourish reaffirms faith and commitment. Like millionaires in the kingdom of God, Conference members raise the roof with sound:

> Let us take up the cross,
> Till we the crown obtain;
> And gladly reckon all things loss,
> So we may Jesus gain.

The Conference elects an annual President who is always an ordained person, either male or female, to hold this honourable position. Following the heroics of their intrepid founder John Wesley, the launched President travels the country ceaselessly, exercising leadership, inspiring vision and proclaiming the gospel of salvation.

Can these bones live?

The audience remains standing as the nominated President is inducted by the retiring President. The Field Bible which John Wesley used is handed on; a symbol of the apostolic succession of the Word. The house lights dim. The President goes to the rostrum. All eyes are upon him. On the huge multi-media screen you can see hesitation in his face. There is nervousness in his voice:

> It is customary to begin the Presidential address by expressing thanks to the Methodist people. This I gladly do for within the Methodist family I have found friends, fulfilment and faith. You have honoured me so that I can honour God, but I can only do this with your prayerful support.

4

As confidence grows, his voice becomes more animated. He talks briefly about the need for theology then launches into his address:

> There is a remarkable passage in Ezekiel 37 picturing Israel as a valley of dry bones. God says, 'Can these bones live?' Some churches appear to have a death wish in their resistance to change. 'Over my dead body' is their slogan.

There are nods of agreement.

> Ezekiel replies, 'O Lord God, you know.' God then says, 'Prophesy to these bones, and say to them: O dry bones, hear the word of the Lord . . . I will lay sinews on you and will cause flesh to come upon you . . . and put breath in you, and you shall live; and you shall know that I am the Lord.' The prophet obeys and there is much rattling, clattering and reconnecting. Note the three stages: the first is about the skeleton, the bringing together of bone to bone. This has been taking place in our Church as we have sought to restructure ourselves and set out priorities. However, although structures, priorities and plans enable, they do not give life. Only the word of God and the Holy Spirit can energize and empower.

The speaker has grabbed the ears of the audience. He is going to say something significant about God:

> The Holy Spirit is rattling our bones! What is the Spirit saying to the Churches? He is calling us to radical change. He is speaking to us about repentance and conversion! God

is telling us to create fresh expressions of Church alongside and within the old, since much of the old, in its resistance to change, will not survive. Life only comes to our dry bones through prophecy, that is speaking the word of the Lord (theology) and through the power of the Spirit (Pentecost). Word and Spirit need each other. When the Word is without the Spirit the Church dries up. When the Spirit is without the Word the Church blows up. When Word and Spirit come together the Church grows up. If we are to come alive, attention must be given to theology and to the work of the Holy Spirit.

If you have not already guessed, I was the newly appointed President. After this introduction I spell out my understanding of the Spirit's person within the Trinity, the world and the Church:

John Wesley said, 'I am not afraid that the people called Methodists should ever cease to exist, but I am afraid lest they should only exist as a dead sect, having the form of religion without the power.' Wesley's fear is now being realized. It is as if we are trying to preserve telephone kiosks in the age of the mobile phone. The Spirit is seeking to make the Church into the vibrant vehicle of God's tomorrow, no longer a museum piece of God's yesterday.

What is mission? 'Mission is seeing what God is doing in the world and joining in.' We in the West have substituted 'Church' for 'Spirit' as the third person of the Trinity

and in so doing have reversed God's understanding of mission. God has a mission; we
are invited through the Holy Spirit to participate in it. When the Church does not join
in with what God is doing in the world then
Church ceases to be Church and becomes a
club. What some view as the decline of the
Church is simply God passing judgement on
nostalgic religious clubs.

No one was dozing off. I saw light in people's eyes
and felt a buzz of excitement rippling through the
audience. When I outlined some structural changes
necessary to unblock the Spirit's work, applause
broke out. The final section entitled 'The Holy Spirit
in us' was more personal:

It is hard for ministers and church leaders
to maintain a passion for God in a declin-
ing Church. Through our struggle to follow
Christ, we become bruised and wounded,
ever aware of our own frailties and failures.
Some of us carry an inner pain too deep
for words. There can be a wilderness of the
heart, a valley of dry bones. Yet this place of
brokenness is the renewing centre of Spirit
and Word.

Ring the bells that still can ring
Forget your perfect offering.
There is a crack in everything,
That is how the light gets in.[1]

As I brought the address to a close, images of a
tranquil sea ebbing and flowing appeared on the
screen. There was the distant sound of waves:

The waves of Spirit are beating on the shore. We sense the restless rhythm of unimaginable depths. God is calling us to launch out into the deep until our feet no longer touch the bottom. But we dare not stop if we are to be sustained by the optimism of grace. The Church in Britain stands on the threshold of a fresh discovery of itself. Come, Holy Spirit. Disturb our complacency. Drive away our fears. Remind us of the faith we have forgotten. Breathe your fluid life into us until the living waters of Spirit well up, washing, cleansing and renewing. Then carry us on the tides of your love into the very mystery of your being.

A profound silence followed. A presence hovered over us. As the audience sang 'Spirit of the living God, fall afresh on me' some wept with emotion. We were on the edge of Pentecost.

Who wants to be a millionaire?

Where did the address come from? It was given to me in a dream. If that sounds too easy I should add that I was only able to receive and digest it because of a lifetime of theological reflection and struggle. Although this book tells the story of how the vision took shape; that is not its main purpose. This book has two aims; first to invite you to become theologians and secondly to encourage you to live on the edge of Pentecost.

Several times the apostle Paul in his letter to the Ephesians mentions the immeasurable 'riches' of grace (1.7; 2.7; 3.8; 3.16) and implies that believers in Christ Jesus are spiritual millionaires:

> I pray that . . . you may know what is the
> hope to which he has called you, what are
> the riches of his glorious inheritance among
> the saints, and what is the immeasurable
> greatness of his power for us who believe
> . . . (1.17–19)

In a further passage he exhorts us to claim 'the
boundless riches of Christ' and prays:

> . . . that according to the riches of his glory
> . . . you may have the power to comprehend,
> with all the saints, what is the breadth and
> length and height and depth, and to know
> the love of Christ that surpasses knowledge,
> so that you may be filled with the fullness of
> God. (3.16–19)

Being a theologian and living on the edge of Pentecostal fullness are part and parcel of our millionaire
inheritance. Word and Spirit make us millionaires.

Who wants to be a theologian?

Paul in these passages is not simply addressing the
clergy or specially trained persons like himself; this
knowledge is a shared wisdom with 'all the saints'.
Paul wants every disciple of Jesus Christ to be a
theologian. It is a crazy idea, particularly as many
ordained ministers do not think of theology in this
way. They cast their minds back to college and associate the word 'theology' with thick dusty books, replete
with complicated ideas, stuffed with footnotes. There
is something very wrong when an ordained person
remarks, 'Of course, I am not a theologian.' I now
reply, 'Then you should not be in the ministry.' Ministers should not project dismal pictures of theology on

to people in the pew. As professionals they blatantly short-change the Church as well as themselves.

Avery Dulles in his book, *The Craft of Theology*, mentions three styles of theology: the propositionalist-cognitive, the experiential-expressive, and the cultural-linguistic. He writes:

> Each of these theological styles has its own view of the nature of doctrine. For the first, doctrines are informative propositions about objective realities; for the second, they are expressive symbols of the inner sentiments of the faithful; for the third, they are communally authoritative rules of speech and behaviour.[2]

To the average churchgoer this use of technical language confirms every suspicion that theology is abstract, obtuse and incomprehensible. This book, though, seeks to open up the closed world of clerical and professional theology so that every Christian can become a spiritual millionaire of Word and Spirit.

Like Dulles I shall play with the theological ingredients of Scripture, experience, tradition, interpretation and Church, tossing in a few extras on the way. My method and conclusion, however, will be very different from his since I shall draw out theology from my own life story rather than seek to construct a comprehensive system of belief for the Church. This is an acceptable approach because theology is testimony; the telling of a story. At its root the word 'theology' literally means 'God-talk' (from the two Greek words, *theos*, translated 'God', and *logos*, translated 'word').

I am inviting you to reflect on your own story as you travel with me on my theological journey. Theology is born out of personal experience reflected upon, checked out and integrated within the wider experience of the Church and the world. We shall discover that Christian theology, although personal, can never be individualistic. We have to be part of other people's stories if we are to be firmly anchored in God's story. The book's purpose is reflected in the subtitle, 'a theological journey of transformation'. Our personal theology is transformed even as it transforms us. Paul wants you to be a spiritual millionaire. It is a crazy idea but not impossible if we travel together.

Pentecost and liminality

Paul mentions 'being filled with the fullness of God'. To make sense of this phrase and with it my interpretation of Pentecost I need to say something about 'liminality', a term with which you may not be familiar. Victor Turner uses this word, previously applied to 'rites of passage', to illuminate the plight of churches.[3] Their marginalized and depressed state, he argues, places the Church on the 'threshold' of what he terms 'reaggregation'. For simplicity I am calling this 'the edge of Pentecost'. It is a place of confusion, a state of betwixt and between. The Church has to lose its identity, becoming invisible within the usual norms of society, before it can be reintegrated as a transforming presence within contemporary culture. The Church moves from being a caterpillar, passing through the pupa stage of liminality to be transformed into a butterfly. Ezekiel's valley of dry bones is a snapshot of 'liminality', a threshold experience of awaiting resurrection and transformation through Word and Spirit.

11

Corporate liminality is accompanied by personal liminality. Personal liminality describes those threshold experiences of transformation which take place from time to time within one's own life journey when we painfully 'cross over' from the old to the new through repentance and faith. The word 'conversion' can be used to describe this. Finding ourselves on a liminal threshold opens us up to the possibility of exceptional and intense religious experience.

Being on the edge of Pentecost and standing on a liminal threshold are one and the same, for both are transforming, enlightening and empowering; the downloading of the millionaire inheritance of God.

The journey

Our personal journey of transformation begins in Part 1 where theology emerges from autobiography. In Part 2 we examine three theologies which I consider to be essential for interpreting Pentecost. Part 3 addresses the question 'What is the Spirit saying today?' At the end of each chapter you will find questions to aid you on your own theological journey. There will also be a 'prompt question' to introduce you to the subject matter of the next chapter.

Finally, I must add a comment about this book's dedication. Some day, I hope the curiosity of my grandchildren will lead them to ask questions about Christianity. I want them to hear God's story through my own personal story. If, in the pages which follow, the story of God the Father, Son and Holy Spirit does not increasingly become the central theme then I have failed in my task. My aim is to write theology, not autobiography. In the words of John the Baptist speaking of Jesus, 'He must increase but I must decrease.'

THEOLOGICAL EXPLORATION

Some starter questions for you and your church before we get down to the real business of doing theology.

- What did you make of the excerpts from the Conference address?

- How do you respond to the idea that you could be a spiritual millionaire?

- What stops you from wanting to be a theologian?

Although you can consider the questions on your own, theology can only really be done in conversation with others. Since each chapter builds on the one before, the questions are best tackled in a discussion group which meets regularly.

Question for the next chapter

How has your early life shaped your understanding of Christianity?

2

Break Out

Graham, Walton and Ward, in their book designed to help us be theologians, speak about 'theology of the heart' and 'narrative theology'.[1] Creative writing, keeping a journal, making verbatim reports, telling stories and parables come within these two categories. However, if these two theological tools only are used, God is reduced to experience, and theology become psychology. They need, as the above writers point out, the critical impact of God's story and the breaking in of the 'strange new world' of the Bible. My next two chapters illustrate how their approach works as my own story and God's story become entwined.

I am devoting two full chapters to my early experience because my grandchildren, Ben and Sam, will have negotiated their own teenage years by the time they read this. Like all of us, they will have had to face the youthful questions about purpose, vocation (future job), relationships and meaning.

Early days

I was born in the pretty village of Kingsbury Episcopi, Somerset. My mother's maiden name was Martha Mounter, but everyone called her Pat. She had two elder brothers, Herb and Robert (Bob). She was a dark, attractive woman who, maybe because of naivety or childhood poverty, was always giving things away to the less well off. Her motto was 'cleanliness is next to godliness' and I suffered from her desire to keep her only child clean and tidy.

My father, Howard, had drive and ambition. He, like his father before him, was foreman of Bradford's Withy Farm. When not managing the factory at Thorney he would be tramping across the vast expanse of the Somerset Levels supervising the work of some 30 men. When calculating their wages I was amazed at his ability to add up three columns of figures at the same time in his head.

We went to the local Methodist Chapel, where I would sit between my parents. My mother would stand and sing. My father stood with sealed lips waiting for the service to be over. I was fascinated with the pipe organ, but only in my mid-teens was I allowed by the possessive organist to play it.

Thomas Hardy and Humpty Dumpty

I had a very secure early childhood with my clever father and affectionate mother. They loved me dearly but I am afraid I constantly thwarted my mother's hopes as I sought to escape her sticky love. When in 1982, following her death from cancer, I stood in the cemetery, memories of Good Fridays came flooding back. I later set these recollections to verse. It was the day when the mums of our village gathered to pick primroses to adorn the family graves:

> The day was Good Friday.
> How well I recall the funereal tone of the
> day.

The switch on the radio was not turned on
And the toys had been all packed away.
There was a reason for this self-denial,
This was Christ's Passiontide.
And this was the day I picked flowers with
    mum.
For someone important had died.

From my earliest days, thoughts of death clouded my happy moments. I enjoyed trips to the cemetery, was fascinated by funerals and often went with my mum to visit the sick and dying.

As an only child, books became my companions. I used to read with a torch under the bedclothes late into the night. In my early teens I read many of the novels of Thomas Hardy and identified with his dark determinism. Later, when studying the laws of thermodynamics I had no difficulty in appreciating 'entropy'. Entropy tells us things run down; that chaos and disorder always increase. Like the Humpty Dumpty of the nursery rhyme, so excessive is the disintegration that no one can put things together again. I therefore expected the worse. Ideas of fate, fall and death appealed to me.

However, when I was recently asked what difference Christianity had made to my life I replied, 'It has replaced my natural pessimism with an optimism of grace.'

First Communion

At the age of 13 I became a church member and took my first Communion. In those days the Lord's Supper was tacked on to the end of the normal service allowing the non-members to leave before the sacred elements were unveiled. As a child I wanted to peep under the white cloth to see if there was real blood there. It was therefore with a sense of anticipation that I waited on the moment when the minister, like some conjurer performing a trick, would reveal all.

I went forward, knelt at the communion rail and held out my hands. A small cube of bread was placed in them which I quickly popped into my mouth. It didn't taste of anything. I was next given a tiny glass of Ribena. I felt very let down. Where was the magic? Then it happened! The ground seemed to shake and ripples of electricity swept through my body. I could hardly stand to return to my seat. I was overawed, terrified, as if struck by a thunderbolt. The whole chapel blazed with white light. I don't remember much else except that afterwards the congregation beat a hasty retreat from the building to stand and gossip outside as if nothing had happened. But something had happened!

That's how my Christian journey of transformation began. What does a young teenager do next? I realized the experience was mine alone but was afraid to tell anyone. The 'happening' hovered on the edge of my being, a secret without interpretation. Surveys have shown how many people have spine-tingling experiences, mediated through music, art or nature; but because they lack a theological interpreter they do not link such experiences with God. I recall other occasions when, as a teenager, I sensed a 'presence' beyond me. Sometimes cycling home late at night under the vast dome of the heavens I would stop in the darkness and gaze in awe at the Milky Way.

You may be able to recall such moments yourself. Nevertheless, we need to remember that it is faith in Christ, not experiences, that makes us Christians.

Music and mystery

Through my mechanical fascination with the church organ I came to discover the music of J.S. Bach. We had no piano, but because I wanted to learn, my parents gave me an old piano accordion. Playing Bach upon it was quite a challenge. I had a fine treble voice and, though it scared me, I enjoyed performing in public. There were also other things to think about, like homework, new friends at Yeovil Grammar School, girls and finding out about sex.

I had a natural curiosity and was always asking 'Why?' I used to take things apart to find out how they worked, so I inevitably puzzled over my experience at Communion. Finally I plucked up courage and asked the minister to lend me a book. He gave me *The Idea of the Holy* by Rudolph Otto. It was not the sort of book you give to a 14-year-old, although I plodded through most of it. When I confessed I had found it difficult, the minister admitted he thought it might be, so he had never read it himself. I did conclude that, like Abraham, Moses and Isaiah, I had been touched by a 'mysterious presence from beyond', something which Otto called 'numinous'. It foreshadowed a special purpose.

Theologians use the word 'transcendence' to describe that which is beyond them. I later came to see that God had revealed himself to me as God – but what sort of God? Not the 'President of the immortals' identified by Thomas Hardy at the end of his novel, *Tess of the D'Urbervilles*, a divine manipulator who plays games with us. No, the God who had come to me was more fascinating and benevolent. Yet it was not possible from the experience to 'read off' the character of this God since the disclosure concealed rather than revealed. It only showed me what God wasn't.

Jesus the friend

At the age of 15 I was given a book of sermons by Leslie Weatherhead and introduced to the writings of C.S. Lewis and William Barclay. In reading them, I now wondered if Jesus could be my friend. The answer was not far away. A tent was erected in a field on the edge of our village and an evangelist arrived for a week's mission. I went along. It was so unlike the rigidity of our Methodist worship. The two testimonies of transformed lives, especially one given by a very attractive teenage girl, were impressive. 'Believe on the Lord Jesus Christ and you will be born again. Do not leave the tent tonight without taking this important step. What would happen to you if returning home tonight you were knocked down and killed?' I had never heard of this happening in our quiet village where only the occasional car or tractor went by though someone had recently been gored by an escaped bull. 'Where will you spend eternity?' he asked. 'Let's close our eyes. If you want to be saved, raise your hand.' People must have raised their hands because he kept saying, 'I see you. Bless you.' I wanted to open my eyes and look. The three people who had raised their hands were afterwards invited to go forward for prayer. I put my hand up on the last evening.

One of Mr Wesley's Preachers

While most of my peer group at Yeovil Grammar
School continued into the sixth form I did not. At the
age of 16 I began an Engineering Apprenticeship with
Westland Aircraft, Yeovil. For the first time in my
life I heard men use swear-words in every sentence,
watched them gamble and saw soft-core pornography
pasted on walls. What a sheltered background I had
had! The next two years were the unhappiest yet. I
left home at six each morning to start work at 7.30.
Eight hours on the factory floor was followed by
night school. I arrived home at 10.15 p.m.; later if I
had to cover the round trip of 20 miles on a bicycle.
Each weekday morning I would wake with dark fore-
bodings contemplating my fate like one of Thomas
Hardy's dreary characters. Was there no escape?

Thankfully, liberation was to come. At the age of 17
I was invited to become a Methodist local preacher.
Here at last was the opportunity I craved. I had a
purpose and a public platform from which to speak.
One of my early sermons on Mark 10.23 showed an
early desire to challenge and disturb:

> Armchair Christians want to sit and there
> are many of them in our chapels. One of
> the tragedies today is that Christianity has
> become socially acceptable. The Church
> is a place where nice people go. Class
> Meetings have gone. Prayer has almost dis-
> appeared. Christian service never gets much
> further than organising a church bazaar, or
> arranging flowers. Christian fellowship has
> degenerated into a nice chat over a cup of
> tea. We have too many respectable people
> in our chapels which resemble social clubs.

> Friend, where do you stand before God? Is
> your religion about the chair or is it about
> the cross?

This was rough stuff, especially coming as it did
from a precocious teenage preacher. I'm surprised no
one complained.

Preaching gave me the incentive to study theology
alongside my night-school disciplines of Mathematics
and Mechanics. I now saw the shop-floor as a mission
field and from my readings of C.S. Lewis sought to
argue the case for Christianity.

The ordained ministry?

Thoughts about the ordained ministry had started to
surface, and they came to a head in the summer of
1957 during a Communion service in a youth camp.
The minister, who organized these annual events,
the Revd Harold Price, called upon those present
to consider a vocation (calling) within the ordained
ministry. We sang:

> Thy life was given for me
> Thy blood, O Lord, was shed
> That I might ransomed be
> And quickened from the dead.
> Thy life was given for me,
> What have I given to Thee?

I went forward to receive the bread and the wine
and responded with the words, 'Here am I, send me.'

I returned home wondering what my parents would
say. My father was silent. My mother cried angry tears
and said I was mad. I cycled to my Uncle Bob's farm.

He told me to feed the cows, climbed on his tractor and roared off to my home. I do not know what he said but I returned to rather chastened parents. My mother was quiet and my father suggested we go for a walk to talk about the practical implications of becoming a minister.

If I imagined it would be a smooth run from now on I was in for a shock. Three days later I received a letter informing me I had won a scholarship to study Engineering at degree level. It would take place through a four-year sandwich course; six months at Westland's to apply the theory and six months at the Northampton College of Advanced Technology (later to be called City University) in London. My father and I made an appointment to see the Personnel Manager at Westland's who was baffled and angered by my reluctance to 'seize the opportunity of a lifetime'. So I accepted my fate and tried to see the scholarship as God's gift. The unresolved vocational tension was to haunt me for the next five years. I wanted to read theology but felt trapped into studying technology. I was angry with God.

Lost in a far country

In January 1958 I left home to live in London on the first phase of my six-month sandwich course of theory and practice. This was to keep me swinging back and forth between independence in the vibrant city of London and small-town existence, living again with my parents.

In my second book on mission, entitled *Into the Far Country*, I emphasize the significance of crossing boundaries. Travelling from one culture or geographical location to another exposes vulnerabilities and opens up the possibility of inner change. There is a real danger of getting lost. Equally, like the lost son in the famous parable (Luke 15.11–32), there is the possibility of 'coming to oneself'. In chapter 1, I introduced you to the idea of liminality (p. 11). My regular six-monthly relocations to and from London for the next five years opened up inner dislocations making me unsure which was 'home' and which the 'far country'. This geographical unsettlement was to lead to a second liminal moment, the first having already taken place when I left school.

London in the late 1950s was a beguiling place for a country lad. There was much to see, exotic places to visit, and attractive women to meet. I was intoxicated with it. When I stepped into my small room, 8 by 10 feet, which was to be my temporary abode for the next three years, I felt fearful but free. I threw myself wholeheartedly into the many delights of London with my new friends; art galleries, cinemas, concerts, late night parties and a chance to do forbidden things.

My obsession with theology remained, however. I read Bonhoeffer's *The Cost of Discipleship* and Paul Tillich's sermons, *The Shaking of the Foundations*. I started to explore ideas which went way beyond the creative liberalism and free thinking of Leslie Weatherhead. In his search for new symbols to describe the Christian faith, Tillich had written:

> Forget all Christian doctrines; forget your own certainties and your own doubts, when you hear the call of Jesus. Forget all Christian morals, your achievements and your failures when you come to him.[2]

I was in the 'letting go' mood and fast embracing existentialism even though I was not sure what it was. (Existentialism is a theory emphasizing each individual as the subject of his/her own existence and destiny.) When someone spoke to us at MethSoc (the Methodist Society) about Bonhoeffer's *Letters and Papers* I was entranced with the idea that we had 'come of age' and could cast off some of the accumulated clutter of the centuries to embrace 'religion-less' Christianity. I was toying with some of the ideas later to be found in John Robinson's *Honest to God*, published three years later.

My belief system then can be summed up in a few slogans:

> God is depth. God is love, love is God.
> Love God and do what you like.
> To know all is to forgive all.
> You are always accepted.

Disturbing cracks were opening up in my person as the various compartments of my existence began to fall apart. Further dislocation was caused by the six-month sandwich course transitions. Where was home? Where was the 'far country'? My parents were baffled by the changes taking place in me. So too were my Christian friends from the village chapels who were alarmed by what I told them. In their eyes I had become a backslider.

President of the Conference?

Not being sure whether I still remained a Christian, I was shocked by a throw-away comment from my college friend, Bill. He often came with me on my sermon-tasting jaunts and we both enjoyed visiting the City Temple to listen to Leslie Weatherhead. On this occasion, the preacher was the Revd Edward Rogers, who happened to be President of the Methodist Conference. At the end of the service Bill turned to me and said, 'One day you will be President of the Conference.' It was a crazy idea.

THEOLOGICAL EXPLORATION

- When, where and how have you had a transcendent experience? What did you make of it?

- How has your early life shaped your understanding of Christianity, Church and religion?

- What difference has Christianity made to your life?

Question for the next chapter

How different is the God discovered in the Bible from the God of Church and religion?

3

God is Dangerous

'God is dangerous.' I used the sentence in my Presidential address. Out of the dozen local radio interviews on the day after my induction, five interviewers latched on to this phrase. I responded by saying that the God of many Christians had been tamed and sanitized, becoming a pale replica of the 'holy God' who shakes kingdoms, remakes churches and turns our lives upside down.

It is not only God who is dangerous. There are dangerous and beguiling places. The 'far country' turned out to be such a liminal place for the prodigal son in Luke 15. Carthage had a similar fascination for the young Augustine (later to become St Augustine), sucking him into a reckless lifestyle:

> I came to Carthage, where there was, as it were, a frying pan full of flagitious loves, which cracked round about me on every side. I was not yet immersed in love, but I desired to be so . . . I despised the way of safety wherein there were no pitfalls. For my soul was famished within me, for want of that spiritual food which is thyself, O my God . . . It was a dear thing to me to love and to be loved, and the more sweet if I arrived to enjoy the person whom I loved.

> I troubled therefore the water of friendship
> with the diet of unclean appetite.[1]

Substitute 'London' for 'Carthage' and Augustine could be speaking of me. I too embraced a heady cocktail of sensuality, spirituality and sexuality. I was hungry for new experiences. I no longer wanted to stay within the confines of my upbringing and the 'be good' morality of the village chapel. I wanted to explore freedom. This invariably led to the painful breaking of relationships and hurting people along the way.

Total collapse

I wanted the best of both worlds. My Christianity was kept in a separate compartment. There was also anger and vocational confusion within, and it was not easy to hold all this together. In the words of Augustine I had become 'an enigma to myself'. I was in a mess and knew it. At the age of 21 my health collapsed. In mid-term I was diagnosed with pleurisy and tuberculosis and whisked off to Paddington General Hospital. Reflecting on this traumatic period two years later I wrote:

> Where is God today?
> He seems so far away
> That he is dead, they say.
> O where, O where is God?

All my securities had gone; my Engineering studies abandoned, my theology in tatters, my call to ministry buried somewhere beneath the collapsed building of a chaotic spirituality. When fully recovered I would have to repeat the year by joining the autumn entry of students. This not only meant an additional year of study but the loss of all my year-group friends. I was also told that whether I completed the course or not, I would have to work an extra year at Westland Aircraft or pay back the thousands of pounds they had spent on me. I was trapped.

The enforced retreat in hospital became a time of reappraisal. Someone gave me a little book by Emil Brunner called *Our Faith*:

> If you really inquire about God, not with mere curiosity, not as it were like a spiritual stamp-collector but as an anxious seeker, distressed in heart, anguished by the possibility that God might not exist and hence all life be one great madness . . . then you already know that God exists . . . you want God because without Him life is nonsense.[2]

This spoke to me. I had put God into a separate 'church' album, treating him as a collectable 'object'. I was guilty of idolatry; constructing my own God of love who condones rather than condemns. My life had become 'nonsense'.

The collapse of one's personal faith is not necessarily a catastrophe. It can become a 'rite of passage'; a 'liminality moment'; a 'transforming event'. Such events are stages on the road to growing up as a Christian. They are not confined to our teenage years, as you will see later. You may be able to recognize such moments within your own Christian pilgrimage.

A dangerous God

I returned home in the summer. One of my friends, Colin, who had gone via the sixth-form to university in Aberystwyth, had fallen under the spell of Calvinism (hard-line exponents of the theology of the sixteenth-century Reformer, John Calvin). Colin raved about a certain Martin Lloyd Jones. During my 'taste a sermon' period in London I had gone several times to hear Lloyd Jones at Westminster Chapel. His sermons always made me angry and on leaving I would vow never to return; but I did. A few weeks before my hospitalization, I had heard him speak about 'the wrath of God':

> For though they knew God, they did not honour him as God or give thanks to him, but they became futile in their thinking, and their senseless minds were darkened. (Rom. 1.21)

During my convalescence I saw how I had tamed the holy God. Memories of that significant 'numinous' encounter at my first communion came flooding back. In my Presidential address when I said 'God is dangerous' I was recollecting this period of my life. In an article for the *Methodist Recorder* I took up the same theme:

> Awe, fear, terror, and shaking; these signal the presence of the Holy One. It is a dangerous thing to fall into the hands of the Living God. The fear of the Lord is the beginning of wisdom . . . Because Christians call God 'Father' and see the friendly face of God in Jesus Christ there is a tendency to dumb down unpalatable aspects of the divine. The

slogan, 'God is love' often reeks of cosiness rather than holiness.

In taming the terror we have lost the wonder. In removing the sharp irritating edges of faith we have managed the mystery. I was brought up on Enid Blyton's book of Bible stories and 'gentle Jesus meek and mild'. When I was converted I met the living God who exploded naïve notions. Mel Gibson's *Passion of Christ,* with all its blood and gore at least messed up the Victorian Sunday School picture of Jesus. A dumbing-down of God invariably takes place when we neglect theology. The result is always idolatry. Reducing God and making gods in our own image is a deadly poison.[3]

During my time in hospital I kept asking, 'How can I return to this living God?' Then an unexpected thought disturbed me. Had God in fact already returned to me in divine wrath? Had he broken out of the theological cage in which I had imprisoned him and pounced like a wild animal? I did not want to contemplate this at the time but have reflected upon it subsequently. Recently I set down a few ideas for an article:

When disaster struck, the ancients saw it as God intervening directly to pass judgement upon godless people. Christians who interpret the Bible literally still see it in this way. Those of a more liberal persuasion with some knowledge of science remove God from such direct action. Because creation has its own independent laws and mechanisms you should not attribute it to God who is love. C.H.Dodd, a New Testament scholar who greatly influenced a past generation of ministers, interpreted God's wrath as 'cause and effect in a moral universe'. When I sin, I reap the natural causal consequences. However, if we recognize the relational nature of our world and how all lives are intrinsically bound together we have to modify this simple cause and effect theory. Issues of global injustice and the growing gap between rich and poor suggest a more complex global network of cause and effect in which others suffer the effects of my sins which may have little or no consequence for me.

Paul did not view God's wrath in an impersonal way. He seems in his letter to the Romans to be suggesting that God's wrath is inseparable from his compassion. God trashes our false religions, idols and absurd behaviour so as to leave us open, vulnerable and exposed to his love, mercy and grace.

God's wrath produces a 'threshold moment' reminiscent of his action in taking Israel into the wilderness to purify her and prepare her as a 'new bride for the Lord' (Hos. 2.14). William Countryman, explaining liminality, writes:

> The border country where we encounter God at the limits of our everyday experience is a frightening place. It has about it an element of death . . . Even if we believe that God is God who has loved us and given us gifts . . . it is still a challenge to look towards the future, to let go of our anxieties, and to live

> actively in the assurance that God . . . will
> continue to love and commune and work
> with us. The HIDDEN HOLY is neither
> against us nor aloof from us, but for us.[4]

Although God is the creator of cause and effect, the manner of Christ's death (the atonement) tells us that God is also the victim of it, since in Christ he too is caught and crushed in the grinding cogs of human sin. Whenever and wherever people perceive God's wrath in events, they are also able to discern his pain.

A fresh start

I needed to make a fresh start. I had lost touch with the Bible and forgotten how it could speak to our condition across the centuries. Conservative evangelical Christians regard the Bible as the Word of God. My liberal reading of Scripture prevented me from embracing biblical fundamentalism where every word is believed to have been dictated by God. Emil Brunner again came to my rescue. Of the Scriptures, he had written:

> The Bible not only comes from Christians;
> Christians come from the Bible . . . The Bible
> is the soil from which all Christian faith
> grows. . . Christian faith is Bible faith.[5]

I knew there was no way in which reason could help me accept the Bible as the Word of God; rather as one becomes a Christian, a 'leap of faith' is required. So I jumped across the reason gap to enter the strange new world of the Bible, which exploded with meaning. Karl Barth describes his discovery, which resonated with mine:

> We read all this, but what do we read
> behind it? We are aware of something like
> the tremors of an earthquake . . . There is a
> river in the Bible that carries us away – once
> we have entrusted our destiny to it – away
> from ourselves to the sea . . . When we find
> God in the Bible, when we dare with Paul
> not to be disobedient to the heavenly vision,
> then God stands before us as he really is.[6]

In January I returned to college. I abandoned
MethSoc, forsook the City Temple and pursued my
lonely labours in Mechanical Engineering. London
had lost its appeal. All my former friends had gone. I
occasionally went to hear Lloyd Jones but found the
Calvinist notion of double predestination, in which
God saves some and damns others, to be obscene. I
wondered how Wesley had dealt with it. I therefore
bought an abridged version of his Journal and made
frequent trips to Wesley's Chapel in City Road.

I now shared a room with a medical student, who
happened to be a Quaker. We spent hours, when we
should have been studying, reading to each other. I
read extracts of Wesley's Journal to him and he read
selections of George Fox's Journal to me. Others in
the house doubted our sanity.

In 1964, the Engineering phase of my life drew to a
close. I had been accepted for the Methodist ministry
and would at last be able to give my full attention to
the study of theology.

Crazy theology

I was bowled over by my first glimpse of Richmond
College, London; its stately grandeur set within

towering trees, evoking memories of missionaries who had gone to distant lands. Full of excitement I strolled down its echoing corridors and stood in awe as Bonhoeffer had before the boards of remembrance in the entrance hall, which listed those missionaries who had died in the service of Christ, some fulfilling only two years' ministry in the 'white-man's grave' of West Africa.

When I actually met the second- and third-year students, my expectations were blown apart. What I found was in stark contrast to the serene surroundings suggestive of prayerful reflection. A theological explosion not unlike a terrorist bomb had hit the community the previous year in the shape of John Robinson's *Honest to God*. Some of the students were boycotting lectures, abandoning prayers and seeking 'worldly holiness'. The main advocates had since left but their turbulent legacy remained.

I had read *Honest to God* six months before and was frankly amazed at the hubbub it had caused in this place of learning. How could theological students not be aware of the book's limitations? Having already pursued some of the ideas of Tillich and Bonhoeffer and ended in a spiritual cul-de-sac, I had no wish to repeat the journey. Even the phrase 'God of the gaps' held no terrors for me. My studies in technology had introduced me to quantum and relativity theory which showed me how the older Newtonian concept of 'space' had to be revised. To argue that God could be pushed out of the world by the advance of science assumed a nineteenth-century world-view now superseded by the 'new physics'. On the positive side *Honest to God* drove me in my leisure moments to read the whole of Tillich's *Systematic Theology* and some of the essays of Rudolph Bultmann. After an initial hesitation I plunged wholeheartedly into theological discussion.

If we are to speak of God to others with conviction and competence, debate is unavoidable. Like Jesus, who was driven by the Spirit into the wilderness, college is an important testing-ground of preparation for public ministry. We learn more from those who disturb us than from those who agree with us. Local churches are not usually theologically dangerous. Maybe this is why we have lost our ability to talk meaningfully about God.

I remain pessimistic about human nature and ambivalent about reason and freedom. If social structures, law and institutions are removed many human beings would quickly degenerate into the savages of William Golding's *Lord of the Flies*, producing a world of chaos. What has happened in Iraq since the US invasion suggests that without these bulwarks of community, individuals do not behave like idealized, freedom-loving Americans. In short, there is something in us which deludes our judgements and releases our primal animal nature; something called 'original sin'.

Looking at God and religious experience through the lens of reason alone always reduces God. Indeed, we become guilty not simply of ignorance but of culpable rebellion, because we dethrone the Creator and invent a fictitious God. Calvin had written, 'scarcely a single person has ever been found who did not fashion for himself an idol or spectre in place of God'.[7]

In my third year, I studied the early Latin and Greek Fathers and the theology of Luther and Calvin. I wanted to learn more about the 'theology of the Word' and find out if Calvin was a Calvinist – which he wasn't – and whether the idea of God's election is fundamental to an understanding of the gospel – which it is.

Calvin with haggis

At college I became engaged to Christine, a Somerset girl with whom I had fallen in love a few years before. We were married in my final year and began to think increasingly about where the Church might send us. Some initial conversation had taken place and South Wales was mentioned. The list of appointments duly appeared on the notice-board. We students scrummed around it. I read the single word 'Armadale' and looked for it on the map. There was no Armadale in South Wales but one on the Isle of Skye. This was not it. My appointment was on the old coaching route midway between Edinburgh and Glasgow. Dismayed, I sought an immediate interview with the resident tutor and asked why I had been sent there. He replied, 'You have studied Calvin. We thought it would be good for you to experience Calvin at first hand.' Such were the ways of ministerial appointment in those days.

In obedience, Christine and I set off for the land of bagpipes and haggis with all our possessions tucked in the back of an Austin A35 van to live in a place we had never seen or even heard of before. After travelling for nearly two days we left the gorgeous Scottish scenery behind and entered a desolate landscape scarred by mining. Our manse looked out on the Atlas Steel Foundry and we were surrounded by 19 factory chimneys. We were greeted enthusiastically by the church ladies who spoke of 'flitting' and used words we did not understand. Their welcome was warm but the place was cold.

That night my wife cried herself to sleep. It was different in every respect from the swinging Kings Road, Chelsea, where she had lived. In my jaundiced moments when looking back at our three years in Armadale I wondered what I achieved. I think the significant contribution was made by Christine who brought the mini-skirt to the town, much to the delight of the youth club. With mature hindsight and following a visit in 2006 I see how God not only reshaped us but blessed us through the friends we made there.

On our first Sunday the small Methodist church was packed to capacity. Many had come to see the 'new minister'. I led the worship and preached. Some of those present never came again. However, an interesting comment made by the steward was later reported to me. 'One day,' he said, 'Tom Stuckey will be President of the Methodist Conference.' It was a crazy idea.

THEOLOGICAL EXPLORATION

- Has your faith ever collapsed? How did it happen and what did you do?

- Is your church a theologically dangerous place?

- What bits of faith, doctrine or creed have you jettisoned? Describe your core beliefs.

Question for the next chapter

How does 'testimony' migrate into 'academic theology'?

Part 2

Doing Theology

4

Cooking the Books

Luke, the author of the Acts of the Apostles, offers us an idealized picture of the Early Church. He unashamedly 'cooks the books' to give us a vision of mission and 'spins' the account to feed us with the Word of God. In his narrative we have stories, history, sermons, conversations, reflections, dramatic actions and testimony all mixed up in a wonderfully creative message about the Acts of the Spirit. 'Doing theology' is a kitchen activity of mixing the right ingredients in their correct proportions and cooking them up into an appetizing meal.

One of Luke's ingredients is the 'sermon'. In this second part of my book I shall focus on the contexts of three of Paul's sermons. First, there is the sermon preached in the synagogue at Pisidian Antioch (Acts 13.14–52) to a congregation of 'insiders' and 'fringers'. Here Paul draws on 'preacher's theology', the subject of Chapter five. Second, Acts 14.8–17 tells the story of how Paul, in a community context, demonstrated the gospel through a powerful deed. We shall examine issues relating to this in Chapter 6. Third, Acts 17.16–34 illustrates how he approaches a very different cultural context in a radical way; the subject of Chapter 7. In Acts 26.1–29 Paul's witness takes the form of 'testimony'; telling his story as I have been telling mine in the last two chapters.

This chapter shows how testimony migrates into theology.

An indigestible meal

Before leaving Richmond College in 1967 I articulated my faith in what I shall label 'my Richmond creed':

> I believe in a mysterious God, hidden and utterly transcendent.

> I believe in Christ, the Word made flesh, the Bible (the written word) and preaching (the spoken word).

> These reveal the mysterious God.

> I believe in God the creator and preserver, who interacts with his creation.

> But creation is spoilt, marred by evil, the devil, and subject to fate.

> It would collapse into nothingness but for God's forbearance.

> I believe in Redemption.

> Through the life, death and resurrection of the incarnate Word there is a new creation.

> God's election through the preaching of the Word brings the gift of salvation to be accepted or rejected by faith.

> I believe in the Church.

> It is the new humanity, the fellowship of believers both in this world and the next.

I believe in the sacraments of Baptism and Lord's Supper.

Baptism signifies grace which is claimed through justification by faith alone.

The Lord's Supper is both a converting and a confirming sacrament of assurance.

I believe in judgement and heaven.

Those never hearing of Christ whose lives demonstrate belief in God may find faith in the end.

Those who hear but reject the gospel will fall into the nothingness from which they were taken.

Predestination describes the assurance of those who persevere to the end.

There are many technical terms here, unlike the scrappy slogans of my 'faith statement' in Chapter 2. If you are uncertain of their meaning it doesn't matter too much. This statement of faith reflects my polemical encounters in college, is unaccommodating and smells of Calvinism. Many traditional creeds of the Church arose from similar conflict situations. Mine is a mechanistic and theoretical creed which only an engineer could produce. It serves, nevertheless, as a marker of where I was on my theological journey. It also helped me face the preaching demands of my first appointment. Did you notice the glaring deficiencies? Notably absent is any reference to the Holy Spirit. Neither is there any suggestion that God might love us.

Where had love gone? C.S. Lewis, whose books I devoured in my teens, had written about the three Greek words for 'love'. I appreciated *filia* (brotherly love and friendship), experimented with *eros* (sexual love) but at the time was muddled about *agape* (the word used in the New Testament to describe God's love). I had been loved but was scared of being trapped. In attempting to preserve my freedom and maintain control I had missed the fragrance of *agape*. I had turned God into an 'object' – a collector's item – and was starting to appreciate that I had treated members of the opposite sex in a similar utilitarian way. This was to change, and the reason was Christine Plympton, my wife, who was henceforth to be my lifelong companion and friend. Although the tension between *eros* and *agape* was not to be resolved for some years, I had started to appreciate *agape* both in other human beings and in God. In 1985 I wrote a long poem in praise of Christine. Here is one verse:

> How mysterious is this woman,
> So ever true yet ever enigmatic.
> I marvel at what has come to pass;
> For I knew not love 'til I knew her,
> And knowing her
> Is love.

In the theological kitchen

How was my Richmond creed produced? If we continue to use the 'cooking' analogy: it depends on the ingredients, their respective proportions and how they are mixed. In part one we have already encountered two essential ingredients: experience and reading.

Francis Young and Kenneth Wilson suggest that John Wesley's progress in understanding the Christian faith came from the 'fruitful interplay of personal experience and wide reading'.[1] This is certainly true of myself as far as it goes yet I must include another ingredient: the significance of parents and friends. Wesley's parents, especially his mother, had an enduring influence upon his theological and personal formation. It is also impossible to ignore the lifelong influence of his brother Charles, other companions like the Moravian Peter Boehler, who pointed him to saving faith, George Whitefield, who later became his sparring partner, and a number of women who befriended Wesley.

My belief system, and probably yours, springs from this testimonial mix of parental influence, relationships with friends, experiences of God and reading. What comes out of the theological oven depends on the proportions of the mix. I had obviously added too much Calvinist chilli powder to make my faith statement digestible, though it did heat up the preaching.

Of course, one can interpret my creed in a secular way, turning theology into psychology. A psychologist looking at my story would probably report:

> Only child – sheltered background – possessive mother – clever father – problems with sexuality – difficulty in establishing loving relationships with women – seeks escape in religion – signs of instability.

> Verdict: some neurosis and risk but not dangerous.

Multiple ingredients

Graham, Walton and Ward have a chapter in their book on the corporate activity of theological reflection and stress the importance of the local congregation.[2] One's personal faith always needs to be challenged and corrected by the insights of others because at its core Christianity is corporate. That is why the questions at the end of each chapter are best considered in a discussion group. The insights of the local church should also be checked out and interpreted within the wider Church and world. The ingredients of Bible, tradition and reason represent this larger theological pool of historic and corporate understanding.

First, the Bible. The Scriptures present a unique challenge since they constitute a library in their own right. Herein are literary forms ranging from history to fiction, legislation to poetry, parable to liturgy, mythology to cosmology. The Scriptures themselves are a cook-book. Are you partial to history, fact, certainty? Is the Bible very important to you? This may lead you to become a biblical fundamentalist. If, on the other hand, you are imaginative, like to question everything and find the Bible of little help, you will probably drift to the more liberal end of the theological spectrum.

I took a leap of faith in accepting the authority of the Bible but am not a fundamentalist with a closed system of thought. Neither do I dismiss great swathes of the Bible as an irrelevance. Paul Ricoeur, who has written much about the interpretation of texts, thinks we spend too much time trying to work out what the author originally had in mind. He maintains that a text has a life of its own and seldom has a singular meaning. Instead, we enter the text as a traveller visiting a far country. We try to live in it for a while until our own world-view is challenged and enriched by the Bible world. To put it another way; I regard the Bible as the Word of God because, through the Holy Spirit, the Word of God, both in the Bible and beyond it becomes the 'living' Word of God for me.

The next ingredient is tradition. I only started to appreciate the importance of tradition when I studied the history of doctrine at Richmond College. The Church's many statements of faith and its development of doctrine is a mixed bag of junk and jewels. One cannot escape making critical judgements. Yet amongst the mistakes and muddles of the historic Church is a rich treasury of faith and wisdom. By dipping into this rag-bag of former centuries I began to appreciate that the faith of the Church was greater than mine. Through encountering the saints, sinners and scholars of the past, God seemed to be saying, 'free up, relinquish control, tune in, learn and become a millionaire'.

The third corporate ingredient is reason. This too is tricky, made more so by the scientific advance of knowledge over the past hundred years. We fondly assume that our generation knows better than previous generations. Ours is a fast-food culture. It is tempting to put the latest pre-packed theological meal in the microwave instead of spending hours in the kitchen sweating over a hot stove. Some convenience foods seriously damage your health. Because we have 'come of age' we are inclined to think that we can jettison those distasteful elements of faith which we have come to regard as obsolescent baggage. But pause for a moment. Why do we assume that a twenty-first-century understanding of God is superior to that of the eighteenth or sixteenth? Certainly, our knowledge has advanced. We have made considerable progress in destroying both each other and the planet. The development of personal freedom and choice has advanced family breakdown and spawned social dislocation, crime and thuggery. We have advanced the gap between rich and poor. We should beware lest our contemporary reinterpretations reduce faith, tame the terror and empty the gospel of its disturbing power.

To sum up: in our theological kitchen, stacked along the shelves, are six ingredients – the influence of parents and friends, experiences of God, the books we have read, the Bible, the corporate faith and traditions of the Church, and the place of humble reason. Within your own theological pilgrimage have you used all these ingredients or are some still missing?

Under the disapproving eye of John Knox

In Scotland I continued my study of the Greek New Testament, attended tutorials at New College, Edinburgh and began a post-graduate thesis on the theology of preaching. Professor Thomas Torrance agreed to be my supervisor. He instructed me to read the first two volumes of Karl Barth's *Church Dogmatics* and attend his lectures because he said 'they do not teach theology in England'.

Twice a week I drove into Edinburgh, climbed the Mound, passed under the austere eye of John Knox and sat in a lecture theatre crammed with students from all over the world as the wonders of *Church Dogmatics* and 'theological science' were expounded. Thus began my lifelong fascination with Karl Barth's *Church Dogmatics* whose lengthy footnotes become dazzling recipes cooked up from the theological ingredients I have described.

I had come to Scotland determined to honour God who, although mysterious and beyond, had revealed himself through his Word. However I was becoming aware of certain difficulties with the idea of absolute transcendence.

If too much emphasis is placed on a God who is beyond the beyond (transcendent) then all we can do is submit to God's inscrutable will. This route took me back either to Thomas Hardy or to Calvinist pre-destination. If disclosure happens only through the 'word' then instead of the Bible why not substitute the Koran, or any other ideological system for that matter? I had chosen 'a leap of faith' into the Bible. What is to stop one from leaping in some other direction? The answer is reason; but reason is distorted and marred by sin. In the final analysis it is a slave of our passions.

I found myself wrestling with the issue of how to avoid what Pope Benedict recently called the 'disturbing pathologies of religion and reason'. Leaps of blind faith into a religious system can place you in the hands of an inscrutable deity, real or imagined, and drive you in the name of God to destructive activity like the suicide bomber.

Barth showed me how the God revealed in Jesus Christ is not only gracious but vulnerable. He is not some impassive distant deity:

> God is now not only the electing Creator, but the elected creature . . . to that extent it includes a self-limitation and self-humiliation on the part of God.[3]

God has renounced the 'form of God' and comes in the 'form of a servant' to humanize us through his weakness and vulnerability. The incarnation, which culminates in the cross, is an exuberant act of folly. God, like a clown in a circus, releases his transcendence through tears and laughter. God's condescension does not generate fanaticism but fun; it is not about crusading but about celebrating; it motivates tenderness not terrorism. Christianity rejoices in life. I learnt this from Karl Barth. Anyone who numbers Mozart as a great theologian, as he does, gets my vote. Towards the end of his life he wrote:

> The angels laugh at Old Karl. They laugh because he tries to put the truth of God in a book of Dogmatics. They laugh because volume follows volume, each thicker than the one before. They say to one another, 'here he comes with his little wheel barrow full of volumes of Dogmatics'. And they laugh about the men who write about Karl Barth instead of writing about the things he is trying to write about. Truly the angels laugh.[4]

Warm theology

In my third year at New College, Father Roland Walls become my supervisor. I had started to question whether Barth's exposition of the Holy Spirit was dynamic enough. My residual Methodism was reasserting itself, breaking open the closed systems of Reformed theology.

As I learnt more about the ingredients and how to mix them in my personal creed, law was giving way to grace, exclusion to inclusion, power to vulner-ability. I realized from my readings of Barth that election within the Bible is a theological concept which proclaims the grace, love and condescension of God while protecting the mystery and holiness of God. All humanity, not some, are elect in Jesus Christ. John Wesley had a more benevolent gaze than John Knox.

Nineteen years after my 'Richmond Creed', I produced another statement of faith:

I believe in God:

the Word, mysterious and beautiful, terrifying yet vulnerable, gracious and compassionate, suffering yet glorious, who for love's sake has limited himself to make a covenant (partnership) with his creation.

I believe in Jesus Christ the Word made flesh:

witnessed to through the written word of the Bible and the preached word of the Church. In his life, death and resurrection he inaugurates a new world calling us to work as his partners in the task of re-creation.

I believe in the Holy Spirit:

the female nature of God inhabiting the earth and all things physical, where human spirituality is renewed in love through our relationships with each other and the earth itself.

But we are ashamed, wear masks and hide our spiritual and physical nakedness.

There are dangers in our exploration of love and intimacy and we are afraid.

I believe in the Church:

the institution where structure must give way to space, where space allows authentic meeting, where true meeting enables new humanity and where the worship of the trinitarian God transfigures the cosmos.

I believe in the sacraments of Baptism and the Lord's Supper:

Baptism identifies us with the new humanity in which divisions in race, sex and wealth are overcome.

The Lord's Supper is both a converting and a sanctifying sacrament of incorporation and liberation.

I have hope in God alone:

who has called humankind, angels and animals to live in harmony with each other and the earth. We are destined to enjoy God.

I believe in risk:

the risk God has taken for us and which I must take if life is to be fully lived and creation restored.

The Japanese theologian, Kosyke Koyama, speaks of 'hot theology' and 'cold theology'. Cold theology is forged in the cool academic atmosphere of reasoned debate. It is a product of the Western Enlightenment (an eighteenth-century philosophy of reason and individualism) which disavows irrationality, paradox and passion. Hot theology is done in the context of poverty, oppression and struggle. It is a Third World product of action and reflection. In Martin Luther's words: 'Not reading books or speculating, but living, dying and being damned makes a theologian.' Theology is not simply about what we write or say; theology is something done!

My theology in Scotland was 'cold theology' but it would warm up! The next few chapters will explain how.

THEOLOGICAL EXPLORATION

- Compare the two statements of faith in this chapter. Where are they different? Why do you think this is?

- In reflecting on your own faith, on which of the theological ingredients do you place your main emphasis? Are there other ingredients which have not been mentioned in this chapter?

- Have a go at writing your own statement of faith. Share and discuss it in the group.

Question for the next chapter

Is preaching essential to the life and renewal of the Church?

5

A Preacher's Theology

For the first time in my life I found myself preaching
every Sunday to the same congregation. At the end of
two months my stock of sermons was used up. The
sermon, for my Scottish congregation, was the focal
point of worship. They listened with rapt attention
though it was impossible to get them to respond
– even with an 'amen'. 'We respond with our silence,'
I was told. Preparation for Sunday now dominated
the week.

Why preach?

In the last chapter I listed six ingredients for the theological meal (p. 48). In this chapter I want to explore
an additional ingredient – preaching. Preaching,
however, is not a simple ingredient; it is a complete
meal in itself. Theology serves preaching. Preaching
feeds the Church.

Paul entered the pulpit of the synagogue in Pisidian
Antioch (Acts.13.14f.) and preached to an expectant
congregation of Jews and 'god-fearing' outsiders. It
was a long sermon based on his audience's familiar-
ity with the Old Testament. The climax was reached
when he triumphantly announced that God in Christ,
through his death and resurrection, had liberated

everyone from bondage to sin. The message caused such a stir that on the next Sabbath the synagogue was packed. There was also an overflow meeting.

English churches in the mid-1960s were not like this. Outsiders seldom attended and the number of the faithful was dwindling. The flickering images of the television had replaced the coal fire to become the focal point of every living-room. Luther's advice of 'stick your eyes in your ears' to those who wished to receive God's message no longer made sense in an age when people were 'hearing' with their eyes. This, along with the heavy demand of sermon preparation, forced me to ask, 'Is preaching rooted and grounded in the purposes of God?' If the answer was 'no', which seemed to be the view of many, then alternatives had to be found.

I remained convinced of my call to preach. It also seemed that preaching, witness and the gift of the Holy Spirit were indissolubly related (Acts 5.32). Karl Barth draws a parallel between the mysterious action of God becoming true man in Christ and the event of preaching.[1] Paul had said something similar:

> Since the world in its fancy wisdom never had a clue when it came to knowing God, God in his wisdom took delight in using what the world considered dumb – preaching of all things – to bring those who trust him into the way of salvation. (*The Message*) (1 Cor. 1.21)

Preaching, it seemed, should not be lumped in the same category as speech making, propaganda, entertainment, communication or education, even though it is all of these. Preaching belongs to an incarnational category of its own because it is rooted in the mysterious elective purposes of God.

Preaching and liturgy

A transforming ecumenical cross-over took place in the 1960s. The Roman Catholic Church started to emphasize the importance of preaching at the same time as the Protestant Churches began to discover the significance of worship. This occasioned a reworking of liturgy. The sermon was now placed near the beginning of worship to become an element within the Ministry of the Word. The congregation's response in creed, offering, intercession, and Holy Communion followed. I had been brought up on the 'music hall' model of worship in which the preacher, like the star of the show, performed at the end. The lessons, prayers, offering and hymns were 'song and dance' routines to warm up the audience. People then left the church (music hall) with the preacher's message ringing in their ears. The response was meant to happen, as it did in Pisidian Antioch, through the conversations which followed.

When I was 15 years old, I was told about Methodism's star preachers, Leslie Weatherhead, Donald Soper and William Sangster. Imagine my excitement when it was announced that Donald Soper was coming to preach in a nearby town. Some local people, including my uncle Bob and my mother, were going to hear him. What a night it was: the air of expectation, the hymn singing, this elegant, handsome man who delivered his message with style and panache. Although my mother and others from the chapel complained afterwards that the pulpit was no place for politics (they voted either Tory or Liberal), I was captivated. People talked of Soper's message for weeks. The 'music hall' pattern of worship worked! In Scotland it was still the norm; I embraced it warmly and have often done so throughout my ministry.

Preaching and teaching

The sermon was also under threat from the educationalists. Latching on to the difference in the Acts of the Apostles between *kerugma* (the apostolic preaching of good news) and *didache* (the teaching),[2] it was argued that the purpose of the sermon within the liturgical 'word/response' pattern of worship was to teach. The sermon, however, is a most ineffective instrument for teaching. It is like throwing buckets of water over rows of narrow-necked bottles in the hope of filling them.

I did not accept this sharp distinction between *kerugma* and *didache*. Preaching makes teaching live. The preacher's power lies 'not in initiation but in appropriation . . . the preacher is not there to astonish people with the unheard of; he is there to revive in them what they have long heard'.[3] Furthermore, preaching is about radical confrontation rather than impartation. It is a subversive activity which seeks to undermine our false presuppositions. The preacher confronts us with the radical nature of our predicament by using a method which is offensive and ridiculous. When Paul preached to the educated elite on the Areopagus, it was not only the message of resurrection which upset them but the act of preaching it (Acts 17.18, 32).

Paul sets out his theology of preaching in 2 Corinthians 4.1–18. The Word of God must be proclaimed simply and plainly (v.2). The preacher refuses to use the methods of the educated, instead he/she embraces foolishness in re-enacting the folly of the cross. Vulnerability and brokenness have to be replicated in the preacher who is smashed like an earthenware jar to reveal priceless treasure within. Communication is God's own business. It is God who 'gives the light of the knowledge of the glory of God in the face of Jesus Christ' (v.6). The preacher proclaims as an act of obedience whether they hear or refuse to hear (Is. 6.10, Ezek. 2.7).

Although Paul believed the Holy Spirit was the divine communicator, it is also obvious from the way he preached and crafted his letters that study, experience and wisdom also shaped what he said and how he said it. As a theologian, the Word dwelt in him richly (Col. 3.16). The prophet Ezekiel does not read the scroll containing 'words from God'; he is instructed to eat it (Ezek. 3.1). The digested Word shapes him into a theologian and preacher able to raise the dead in a valley of dry bones.

Preaching and action

In my young days I often heard the saying 'sticks and stones may break my bones but words can never hurt me'. It is untrue. To hear your doctor say, 'You have cancer' will change your life. Some messages have not lost their power.

Unlike the Greek term for 'word', *logos*, the Hebrew *dabhar* represents speaking which is not moderate but 'hot', explosive and revolutionary. *Dabhar* can be translated as 'saying'. 'event' or 'thing'. It not only has intellectual content, it has 'physical' substance because the person speaking the 'word' actually communicates his or her own 'being' and 'person'. Thus God creates by speaking (Gen. 1.3). The Old Testament prophets not only comment on history, they make history. Jesus in his Nazareth sermon reads the Scripture, the 'written word', and by speaking makes it into a 'living word' (Lk. 4.21). It becomes true in their hearing and provokes a riot. A similar uproar follows Paul's sermon at Pisidian Antioch (Acts 13.14–52). To put this in rather a crude way: the preacher is not firing blank cartridges to wake us up from our slumbers, the preacher is shooting real bullets.

Preaching is a product of a Hebraic understanding of the word. Its origin does not come from the Hellenistic tradition of rhetoric, education and illumination. It is not a question of actions speaking louder than words but rather of word and act coming together in the preacher and congregation through the elective work of the Holy Spirit in an explosion of power.

> Why do people in church seem like cheerful brainless tourists on a package tour of the Absolute? . . . Does any one have the foggiest idea of what sort of power we blithely invoke? . . . The churches are children playing on the floor with their chemistry sets, mixing up a batch of TNT to kill a Sunday morning. It is madness to wear ladies' straw hats and velvet hats to church; we should all be wearing crash helmets. Ushers should issue life preservers and signal flares; they should lash us to the pews.[4]

Preaching is an incarnational act in which the Word of God again becomes en-fleshed.

> We do not repeat or imitate the cross on the one hand; and we do not merely state it on the other. It re-enacts itself in us. God's living Word reproduces itself as a living act. It is not inert truth but quick power.[5]

Preaching as dialogue

According to the Old Testament theologian Walter Brueggemann, ours is a monologue culture in which people have become quiescent and isolated.[6] Constant exposure to electronic prattle withers the human spirit. Government, media and advertising bombard us with information and propaganda packaged with the shrill voice of certainty. Market research, consultation, even democracy, create the illusion of dialogue but without removing us from being passive consumers. The Church has long embraced this monologue culture with dead sermons.

Fred Craddock speaks of preaching as 'overhearing the Gospel'. He gives a simple illustration of how he sat behind two people in a bus. They were engaged in deep conversation. Because they were talking about something important his ears pricked up. He wanted to know what happened next; he even wanted to join in. This was something different from those annoying half-conversations bellowed on mobile phones.

Preaching, properly understood, opens a transforming three-way conversation between God, preacher and congregation. It becomes a type of liturgical prayer overheard by the congregation in which God and preacher converse; a bit like overhearing the prayer of Jesus in John 17. We, the congregation, are sucked into the dialogue to become active participants in the drama of the gospel.

You may not be a preacher, and you may be thinking 'What has all this to do with me?' Remember that each of us as a witnessing Christian is required to speak about God in a meaningful and authentic way as part of our discipleship. This chapter suggests that what you say and how you say it really does affect people. God uses our words as a vehicle of transformation through the Holy Spirit who imparts them at a deep level. Remember, too, that as a member of the congregation you invariably hear lots of sermons. How you listen and how you respond can help or hinder the communication process taking place between God, the preacher and those sitting near you.

Seeing stars

I was preaching in Newcastle on Sunday, 11 September 2005. The small congregation was warm, responsive and expectant. Afterwards my friend Leo said I should have asked members of the congregation who wished to rededicate themselves to physically come forward and kneel at the front. Although I replied, 'I don't do altar calls', it got me thinking.

In the evening we went to East Durham, passing the Angel of the North to join a large congregation at Trinity, Shiny Row. I preached on 'Seeing Stars':

> My text is from Genesis 12: 'And the Lord said to Abraham "Leave your country, your people, your father's household and go to the

land that I will show you. And I will make
you a great nation and I will bless you.'"
The word 'blessing' is about flourishing.
Is God blessing you? When were you last
aware of the presence, vitality and energy
of God within? Abraham was someone who
was always having conversations, even argu-
ments with God. During this year I found
myself doing the same.

In my sermon I explained how Abraham took a risk
in stepping out into the unknown. I said I believed we
should do the same. I gave examples of people doing
scary things even in old age:

Jesus commended people who took risks and
exercised faith, but I notice they were nearly
all 'outsiders'. Why is it that we 'inside'
people are so reluctant to do new things? Is
it because we are always looking back? Is it
because we are always looking down? God
instructed Abraham, 'Look up and see the
stars.' God's blessings exceed their number.
So Abraham looked up, believed and became
a millionaire.

I concluded by exhorting the congregation to look
up and become aware of the great cloud of witnesses
cheering them on to claim the blessing:

They're even now encouraging you to step
out; to run the race looking to Jesus, the
author and perfecter of faith. Abraham saw
the stars and stepped out in faith. Will you
step out and do the same?

As we sang I saw the stars too and, overwhelmed with
a sense of awe and wonder, knelt at the Communion

rail with others from the congregation who had come forward to rededicate their lives to God. The miracle of preaching still happens.

Message to preachers

If everyone is to speak of God in a meaningful way, then the renewal of preaching and theology is essential. Like Ezekiel we must eat the Word before we can speak it. This thought lay behind the Presidential letter which I sent to newly accredited Preachers in the Methodist Church. It sums up my theology of preaching:

> Dear Preacher,
>
> The apostle Paul, writing to the Thessalonians Christians rejoiced that 'Our gospel came to you not simply with words, but also with power, with the Holy Spirit and deep conviction' (1Thess. 1.5 NIV). You have now joined the great company of preachers, successors to the apostle himself, and it is a particular privilege to welcome you into that fellowship within the Methodist Church. Ours is a high calling and an awesome task as we attempt to unfold the written word of the Bible so that it can become a 'living word' of power.
>
> If the Church is to recover its confidence and effectiveness in witness, two things are essential: Word and Spirit. Whether you like it or not, as a local preacher you have to be a 'theologian'. People often associate 'theology' with obscurity, thick books and

academic remoteness. For me 'theology' is 'conversation about God'. We Methodists, I am sad to say, have lost our ability to talk about God naturally and in a way which makes sense to people outside the Church. This has to be a priority. Ministers and local preachers are key players here. We are called to feed spiritually hungry people with the living Word of God. We must not give way to the temptation of dishing out junk food. Theology is the kitchen in which we prepare the banquet.

Paul reminds us that if the word is to be a 'living word' it must be empowered by the Holy Spirit. God's Spirit moves more powerfully in situations soaked in prayer. I remember some advice given to me in my early years as a local preacher: 'Think yourself clear' and 'pray yourself hot'. Even though I would not express it like that now, what was suggested still rings true. So keep your thinking sharp through theological study and keep opening yourself up to the Holy Spirit in repentance and faith.

You have a high calling as a local preacher. You are part of God's team shaping the future. Go to it, in the name of Christ, and may he bless you richly.

Tom Stuckey

Moving on

In 1971 we rattled down to Bristol in our battered A35 van, which was belching smoke and dripping oil. In the back were two small boys, Martin and Matthew. Our enlarged family was returning to within 50 miles of where Christine and I had been born. While packing my books in readiness for the move south I came across my 'Richmond creed'. I noticed there is no mention of the person and work of the Holy Spirit. I erased some of the Calvinistic overtones and added the sentence:

> I believe in the Holy Spirit who empowers preaching to renew the Church, enable prayer and equip God's people for ministry.

We little anticipated, as we drove through the night that we were journeying to the 'edge of Pentecost'.

THEOLOGICAL EXPLORATION

- Have you heard a 'good' sermon lately? What made it good?

- If preaching is to become effective, what changes must take place (a) for the preacher, (b) for the congregation, (c) for you personally?

- When did you last speak about God to someone outside the Church? How did the conversation go?

Question for the next chapter

What difference does the gift of the Holy Spirit make?

6

A Charismatic Theology

The sun shone as we drew up outside the Methodist Church in Hartcliffe, a post-war council estate on the south side of Bristol under the verdant slopes of the Dundry Hills. It was an attractive 1950s building with a manse attached. This was to be our home for the next six years. Like Paul in Lystra, the gospel was to make an impact here through a mighty act of the Holy Spirit (Acts 14.8–18).

Vibrancy and vagrancy

Youthful energy and vitality bubbled everywhere in this community, where 40 per cent of the population was less than 20 years old, and only 22 per cent over the age of 45. Hartcliffe swarmed with children. In summer, jangling ice-cream vans perpetually roamed the estate. Teenage mums yelled at their kids, many replicating the experience of their own mothers, who could sometimes be seen through open doorways looking the worse for wear after a wild night. Teenagers in gangs scoured the streets; noisy but not dangerous. Dogs hunted in packs, sometimes terrorizing children. One couple kept a horse in their bedroom.

People had their own values and comparisons. Some expressed resigned loathing, 'I 'ate this bleedin' Grove!' Others, like communal vagrants, were continually on the move from one area to another, always waiting for the next transfer to an imagined shangri-la. It seemed that nearly everybody took drugs – not hard drugs, but antidepressants and prescribed pills to keep themselves going. Hartcliffe was a place of transparency, warmth and friendliness. Our two boys went to the local school and our daughter Joanne, who was born in Bristol, attended the church play-group. For us Hartcliffe was home and since we were young, keen and energetic, we revelled in it.

God's mission

In Scotland the church had been the focus of my ministry. After 18 months in Hartcliffe, the community was setting the agenda. The first requirement of mission is 'presence'. Unlike the hundreds of teachers, social workers and health-care workers who invaded the estate each week servicing its needs, I lived here. This meant a constant trickle, day and night, of desperate people knocking on the manse door. It became impossible to walk down the street in a dog collar without getting caught up in people's muddles. Chris and I were not able to respond to every problem, and it was slowly dawning on me that it was not just the people but rather the place which exacerbated the difficulties.

What are the social dynamics and politics of a 'sink estate'? How does one manipulate the levers of power to bring release to the captives? There were theological questions too. Where is God? What does the Bible say? The second question was easy since one passage in Scripture jumped out:

'The Spirit of the Lord is upon me because
he has anointed me to bring good news to
the poor. He has sent me to proclaim release
to the captives and recovery of sight to the
blind, to let the oppressed go free, to proclaim the year of the Lord's favour.' (Luke
4.18–19)

I was familiar with the more secular interpretations
of the text which propelled ministers into community
development and local politics as a way of releasing the
captives. Our Methodist church was certainly 'doing
its bit'. The church bustled with activities throughout the week and we supported many community
projects. I was also involved in schools' work, other
LEA projects and spent hours at the Housing Depart-
ment. This barely scratched the surface. If Luke's
text was to come true in Hartcliffe, something quite
extraordinary had to happen. People were trapped
externally by the social dynamics of the estate and
internally by their own feelings of defeat, worthless-
ness and marginalization. Furthermore, those of us
who were trying to make a difference were becoming
drained by the perpetual demands.

Hitherto I had overlooked the words 'Spirit' and
'anointed' in the Luke text. Now I noticed that when
Spirit and Word came together things happened.
Jesus' sermon in the synagogue confirmed my own
'preacher's theology', but in Hartcliffe a preacher's
theology was not enough. It didn't work for Jesus
either because he could perform no deed of power
(*dunamis*) 'because of their unbelief' (Matt. 13.58). A
breakthrough could only come in Hartcliffe if there
was some additional resource to stoke up the fires of
faith and give all of us a lift. This 'something' was

not money or additional personnel, though both were sorely needed.

The Hartcliffe people, who were becoming my friends, had to be released from the black hole of despair and given hope. A preacher's theology, the product of 'orthodoxy', did not touch them. 'Orthopraxy', which emphasized the importance of doing the deeds of the kingdom of God, though essential, was exhausting us. What was required was 'orthopathy'.[1] The Methodist theologian, Theodore Runyon, describes this as a transforming religious experience in which the Spirit penetrates the heart, the affections and the will, re-energizing people with a passion to speak and act. Charismatic theology is a radical, indigenous theology of liberation. Or if we avoid the jargon: charismatic theology takes the needs, the context and the culture of people seriously and releases them absolutely.

Sadly, the word 'charismatic' (from *charismata* = spiritual gifts) has become a label applied to 'happy clappy' self-indulgent singing supported by naive theology. Such 'dumbing down' is a symptom of the privatization of religion which has occurred since the 1970s, turning charismatic theology into a travesty of itself.

Adolescent theology

Karl Barth believed that theology becomes a liturgical offering to God when it is done in faith. Since revelation is an act of grace, theology without prayer loses touch with truth. Doing theology is not so much a matter of learning but a manner of praying. At the end of his life Barth said he wished he could begin his own theological work again but starting this next time round with the third person of the Trinity.

My foundational experience of God, my Methodist background and recent theological studies were leading me to the person and work of the Holy Spirit. I set aside more time to pray. Maybe this was why I began to bump into ministers of different denominations who spoke of the charismatic movement.[2] I also met a few people who raved about 'speaking in tongues' (*glossalalia*). One of them had a 'hot line' to God whom, she claimed, spoke to her daily through dreams, pictures and even voices. It was most unsettling. Such spiritual claims are dangerous because reason is displaced by intuition, and doctrine subverted by feeling. The Holy Spirit is being used as a theological labour-saving device. I decided to seek out credible information about the charismatic movement.

Unlike Pentecostalism, which was born in Azusa Street, Los Angeles, this new movement had no single geographical point of origin but was springing up quite spontaneously within and across the Christian denominations of the rich West. It had no 'founders', spiritual centre or mature theology of its own. Its theology appeared to be simplistic and adolescent. In a memo to myself I wrote:

> The Holy Spirit only seems to work after one is baptized in the Spirit; what about prevenient grace and the Spirit's work before conversion? Can you be baptized in the Spirit without 'speaking in tongues'? Is the gift of 'holiness', as described in some of Charles Wesley's hymns, the same as 'baptism of the Spirit'? Some charismatics treat the rest

70

of us as 'second-class' Christians; are we really missing out? How can the charismatic movement be of God if it is fragmenting traditional Churches? Why are charismatic Christians so insensitive to others?

A Roman Catholic priest helped me with some of these questions. He believed the movement was phase two of a worldwide ecumenical movement. It was God's answer to prayers for a New Pentecost. God, he said, is not creating a new charismatic Church but rather charismatically renewing the traditional Churches. The spiritual gifts (*charismata*) are being given to empower the Church's mission of worship and witness.

Man Alive

Working 14 hours most days, I seldom took time off. I was like a circus juggler spinning more and more balls in the air. Soon I would drop the lot. Ministerial demands marginalized my wife and family. My spirit was draining away, my judgements were becoming flawed and my emotional boundaries eroding. I was living on adrenalin.

The Easter ecumenical mission, entitled 'Man Alive', nearly killed me. I found myself lumbered with everything; even getting the donkey for the Palm Sunday procession. Throughout the Lenten period of 1973 I was being broken. Having already stumbled as a teenager through a number of threshold experiences (liminality), I had naively assumed that my spiritual and theological journey would continue without further dislocations. There would be crises and struggles, certainly, but no more radical upsets. You might think the same. If at this stage on my journey I had read about James Fowler's six stages of faith, I would have realized that further painful transitions are necessary if we are to enter into our full inheritance of faith. I was to learn in Bristol that inner broken-ness is a necessary prelude to spiritual renewal. I was to discover, as you will see in the next chapter, that one's theology has also to be broken open. Only theo-logical and spiritual brokenness will take the Church, as well as its people, to the edge of Pentecost.

It was my thesis on preaching which came to the rescue. The Hebrew *ruach* (Spirit) just like *dabhar* (Word) was not to be understood in some meta-physical way. *Ruach* was Spirit and event. The Holy Spirit, although being the 'shy' member of the Trinity, always had a physical manifestation. When closely linked with *dabhar* this manifestation was prophecy. If preaching was to become prophetic, the preacher's theology needed charismatic theology. 'No prophecy ever came by human will, but men and women moved by the Holy Spirit spoke from God' (2 Pet. 1.21). Prophecy according to Paul is the highest spiritual gift within the hierarchy of gifts. (1 Cor. 14.1):

> God has appointed in the church first apos-tles, second prophets, third teachers; then deeds of power, then gifts of healing, forms of assistance, forms of leadership, various kinds of tongues. (1 Cor. 12.28)

I felt I was already displaying some evidence of the gifts of teaching, assistance and leadership. I was not sure if they were natural endowments or gifts bestowed through ordination. The distinction does not matter. According to the theologian Jürgen Molt-mann, whatever one does in the name of Christ is charismatic since the *charismata* and the fruit of the Spirit are expressions of obedience.[3] If Paul is here describing an essential package of gifts required for effective mission then we were seriously missing out!

Should one pray for the gifts one needs? By no means! Gifts are of grace; freely chosen and given by God who apportions as he wills. Nonetheless we can and should pray for more of the Holy Spirit who bestows gifts.

> Come Holy Ghost, our souls inspire
> And lighten with celestial fire;
> Thou the anointing Spirit art,
> Who dost thy sevenfold gifts impart.

Speaking in tongues

I regularly attended a doctor/clergy group. We had a session on 'speaking in tongues' (*glossalalia*). Most people were antagonistic, though one doctor approached the phenomena differently: 'It could be a cathartic way of venting inner pain,' he suggested.

An Anglican priest commented, 'In Gregorian Chant the vowels are so lengthened that the words are meaningless and become vehicles of sound. In prayer and praise how much does language matter?'

'What about the Jesus Prayer of the Eastern Church?' asked another. 'The same phrase is repeated over and over again until it becomes a heartbeat of Spirit and breath. I use this method in approaching contemplation.'

We next discussed methods of praying and a Roman Catholic priest said a similar thing could happen when using the rosary. 'Was speaking in tongues,' he asked 'a method of vocalizing sighs "too deep for words" (Rom 8.26)?'

We concluded that *glossalalia* could be an intermediate phase of contemplation between articulate speech and silence. Although this was not what Paul taught I warmed to it. The transcendent dimension of my own theology suggested that God was unknowable. 'Speaking in tongues' could be a prayerful way of expressing the inexpressible mystery of God to God.

Only intellectual pride now stood in the way. Having confessed this I spoke in tongues a few weeks later while using the 'Jesus prayer'. The Spirit rose like a spring of living water within; washing, cleansing and renewing. The filling did not stop but bubbled over my tongue in praise. The strange language had meaning before it faded. 'Trust in me. The Church is not yours. I will build it and the gates of hell will not prevail against it.'

We want it too

A week later while making a pastoral visit something in my head seemed to whisper, 'Visit Jean' (I have changed the name). She was a church member who seldom attended worship. Should I ignore this intuitive flash? I found her address. She was a receptionist at the doctor's surgery, and I suspected she would not be at home. There was a long delay before my knock was answered. She stood looking guilty, a bottle of tablets in her hand.

'How did you know?' she mumbled.

Once inside, her unhappy story tumbled out. She was going to overdose. Her daughters would not be home for hours.

'You need Jesus in your life,' said I, surprising myself by the language I'd used.

'Yes please,' she replied.

So I laid hands on her head and prayed. After about a minute she said, 'Wow!' I left her sitting in the chair and returned home. Jean later told me how she sat for hours, afraid lest the peace which had flooded her evaporate.

That evening the manse doorbell rang. Jean's two teenage daughters stood facing me.

'I don't know what you did to mum,' said the 18-year-old, 'but we want it too.'

That's how God's mission in Hartcliffe moved up a gear. Within weeks, Jean, her daughters, her sister, her mother and her father (who reckoned himself an atheist) appeared at worship and continued to attend each Sunday. They had all become Christians. Other's joined them. Jean, as a doctor's receptionist, used to say to people requesting repeat prescriptions: 'Have I told you what God has done for me'? So she told them.

Have you too reached that liminal moment in your own pilgrimage when you can say 'I want it too'?

Power tools of mission

The *charismata* are the transforming power tools of mission. They are not optional extras to normal church life; they define normal church life. Both gifts and fruit are essential if the Church is to soar. The energy released is more like the fusion of a hydrogen bomb than the warm feeling one gets after a good lunch. The *charismata* also open up a multi-dimensional 'spirit world' of good and evil forces. The 'principalities and powers' (Eph. 6.12) which my free-thinking, liberal theology had excised (demythologized) were in fact disturbing realities not so easily dismissed.

What gave charismatic theology 'the edge' in Hartcliffe were the social charisms of 'forms of assistance' (1 Cor. 12.28), healing, generous giving, and cheerful compassionate service' (Rom. 12.6f.). Paul insists that these practical charisms be demonstrated. He therefore collects money from the rich churches to give to the poor in Jerusalem as an expression of solidarity and justice. Fellowship (*koinonia*) is not about drinking tea in a church hall after worship; fellowship is justice in action through prayerful and practical economic sharing. Paul criticizes the Corinthian Christians because of their failure to exercise the more practical social gifts of the Spirit which demonstrate justice to the world.

The pursuit of justice is theologically charismatic because it springs, not from social or political motives, but from an understanding of the grace of the Lord Jesus Christ who although 'he was rich, yet for your sakes he became poor, so that by his poverty you might become rich' (2 Cor. 8.9).

A different context

In 1976, we left Hartcliffe to move to Exeter, where I was to be minister of the Mint Methodist Church; a central church with a glorious tradition of preaching and influence. Included in the appointment was a part-time chaplaincy at the University. The cultural leap from a struggling congregation on a council estate to a successful professional church in a historic city poses a considerable challenge. Prosperous churches are often bemused by talk about the marginalized and can cramp a minister's style. It was also obvious that any charismatic dimension in ministry would not be welcomed by the majority. As a result, much of my Bristol experience was placed in cold storage as I colluded with the culture of the church.

Nevertheless, there was a positive legacy. During my Presidential travels around Britain I bumped into former MethSoc students; some of them now Methodist ministers. The secret *charismata* were at work even within my compromised theology and ministry.

In a successful church it is easy to forget God's millionaire inheritance. If a full complement of the fruit and the gifts of the Spirit define normal church life then there are many traditional churches, both large and small, not cashing God's growth cheque. In Bristol my spirituality was transformed. In the next chapter we will see how a change of context can trigger a liminal shift in theology.

THEOLOGICAL EXPLORATION

- As a Christian, what endowments or gifts has God given you. How are you attempting of use them in fulfilling Luke 4.18–19 (page 68)?

- Without the powerful preaching of the Word and the *charismata* of the Spirit, can a church grow?

- An empowering experience of God can make you a more effective witness. Do you believe this? Do you personally want it to happen?'

Question for the next chapter

Where is God at work in the world?

7

A Global Theology

The account in the Acts of the Apostles of Paul's stop-over in Athens is a snapshot of his theological development since Lystra. At Lystra he could barely find words to restrain the superstitious crowd. In the Mars Hill University of Athens he welcomes the opportunity of reflecting theologically with articulate and sophisticated philosophers. He quotes a pagan poet (Acts 17.28). He does not begin with what he has read but rather with what he has seen. His message is not about the Christ who liberates believers from slavery to Moses (Acts 13.39), but rather about 'a man' who frees all people from ignorance. Put simplistically, the message to the Jewish insiders is about salvation, while the message to the Greek outsiders is about illumination. More intriguing still is the fact that Paul begins by speaking of an 'unknown God'. What is crucial about this approach is his willingness to take seriously the context, the culture and the belief system of a very different audience.

It used to be argued that he made a theological mistake in doing this because few were converted. It is now acknowledged that, far from abandoning this method, he embraced it wholeheartedly; indeed Acts 17.16–34 has been called the greatest missionary document in the New Testament. Paul's Jewish theology had become a global theology. This chapter describes how a similar liminal shift occurred within my own theology. My purpose is to encourage you to go beyond your existing theological box.

A multi-cultural context

In 1982 we moved to Manchester. Our eldest son, Martin, was 14, Matthew 12 and Joanne 10 years old. The timing was unhelpful for us as a family; nevertheless the move gave each of us an opportunity to reassess. Christine took full advantage of this by embarking on her training as a nurse.

I had been appointed to the Lewins Chair of Applied Theology at Hartley Victoria College within the Northern Federation for Training in Ministry; an ecumenical set-up of Methodist, Baptist, United Reformed, Unitarian and Anglican Churches. I also had pastoral responsibility for a small, multi-racial church at Manley Park on the edge of the inner city. Our move to this vibrant metropolis occurred in the aftermath of the riots which had erupted in Moss Side the previous year. This post-violent context was to heat up my lukewarm theology.

Like Hartcliffe, Moss Side was a forgotten place for the marginalized. Unlike Hartcliffe there were no green hills in the distance and many of the inhabitants lived like battery hens in ugly crescents and tower blocks. Here was a concrete jungle with a potent racial mix; an urban time bomb waiting to explode. Moreover the deprivation clock had been ticking away since my arrival in Hartcliffe 13 years before and the polarizing policies of Margaret Thatcher had precipitated further despair. Violence was inevitable.

The Church and poverty

Ignition had taken place in Brixton and spread to Moss Side, Liverpool and Birmingham. The Scarman Report, commenting on the events in Brixton, rejected the conspiracy theories of the Government. These urban explosions exposed an enormous comprehension gap between people in the inner cities and the Government whose law enforcers symbolized white authority and racism.

A Christian Aid study, published a few years later, examined the churches' attitude to poverty. Although Christians in Britain acted benevolently towards the poor in other countries, picturing them as victims, we have little sympathy for the poor in our own country. We give them the label of drug abusers, troublemakers, single parents, layabouts and spongers.

In spite of my Hartcliffe experience I had attached little importance to structural justice issues. The charismatic theology which dangled loosely on strings around the neck of my preacher's theology was found to be wanting. My understanding of mission was pastoral and individualistic. I had swallowed the naive theological fantasy that society could be saved through more and more people becoming Christian. The growing polarization between rich and poor in Britain and across the world made this palpably untrue. Like the majority of Christians in Britain I had closed my eyes to the malignant reality of the 'principalities and powers' who incarnate themselves in economic and political structures. Most churches, said the Report, have reduced mission to encouraging 'spiritual development, through prayer, fellowship and worship' and therefore fail to do battle against injustice. We substitute 'charity' for 'justice'. The Church in Britain is guilty of complicity and sin.

Hugo Assman, a liberation theologian from Latin America, has written:

> If the historical situation of dependence and domination of two-thirds of humanity ... does not become the starting point for any Christian theology in the rich and dominant countries as well, theology will no longer be able to locate and give specific historical expression to its basic themes.[1]

He is saying that western theology can only become authentic when it embraces an active attack on global injustice.

A global understanding of mission

Some of the students in college were eager to wrestle with these problems. They did not sit, as I had done 20 years before, waiting like empty vessels to be filled with learning. For the first two years I scurried along, one lesson in front of them, the curriculum in one hand and a bat to field their googlies in the other. Within my course on the 'theology of mission', issues of poverty, justice and evangelism emerged quite naturally. I was learning with and from the students. I remember asking 'Do we take Christ to the world or is he there already?' This led to further questions:

> Where is God in Moss Side?

> Will God by-pass the Church in Britain to bring liberation to the world?

> What is so special about Christianity? What about the other Faiths?

Hitherto my theological pilgrimage had been 'church centred'. The statement 'there is no salvation outside of the Church' had been drilled into me from my early studies, but the inability of the Western Church to come to terms with the scandal of poverty and the curse of injustice was making me doubt this. A significant shift was taking place in my thinking. God was ceasing to be an 'ecclesiastical God' and was becoming a 'global God', concerned not only with individual salvation but with universal humanization.

My understanding of mission and evangelism was trapped within Western cultural assumptions. Miguez Bonino, an Argentinean theologian, challenged our missionaries in 1971 with the words: 'This is my message; Go home and die and come back afterwards.'

Into the far country

If features of the Western Church have to die before we are capable of embracing a different understanding of ourselves what should I be doing as a trainer of ministers? Where must I go to gain this new vision? The phrase 'overseas missions' still conjures up the image of the nineteenth-century missionary hacking a path through the jungle. How is this perspective going to be changed at the local level? And what about you? What sort of understanding do you have?

Study leave during 1987 gave me the opportunity to explore. The book *Into the far country*, written on my return, sets out what I discovered. To catalogue the stories, events and experiences of my three months in India and war-torn Sri Lanka would require another book, for the trip became a spiritual and theological journey of transformation.

I travelled thousands of miles on public transport, mostly without a guide. My itinerary became increasingly flexible as arrangements made in advance failed to materialize. Often uncertain where I would spend the night, I had to trust the stranger. The language barrier made me vulnerable. Although twice robbed and once laid low with fever my lasting impression is one of freedom and joy. I discovered hospitality, generosity and grace in the most unexpected places. Bereft of external props I had to trust God implicitly:

> Living constantly with the contradictions of Asia makes one's tolerance levels grow. You start to live truly in the present with one's body and spirit as well as one's mind. You learn to trust and live with vulnerable openness. You learn a new solidarity which transcends self-sufficiency. You learn that possessions are not really important for everything is gift. You discover joy.[2]

Dialogue with life

One encounter was life-changing: my meeting with Father Michael Rodrigo. He was formerly a Professor at the Roman Catholic Seminary in Kandy. Following study leave to complete his second doctorate in Paris, he found settling back into the seminary difficult because he now believed theology was only credible when done for the people and by the people. He was critical of Western approaches to dialogue between faiths which he held to be elitist. Dialogue recovers its integrity only when it takes place in the context of struggle, suffering and death; passing over from power to weakness, from words through action to silence. This calls for a discipleship of a most sacrificial kind.

Michael abandoned everything to go and live with
oppressed farmers in the wilderness of Lower Uva,
where 99 per cent of the inhabitants were Buddhist.
In the face of the suffering poor he beheld the face of
God:

> The poor are not objects of pity but subjects
> of their God-given destiny, for with us or
> without us they will arise as Christ arose.
> For God uses the weak to confound the great
> and equips the foolish to break the shackles
> of the proud.

The Church in this hostile environment was visible
only through the quiet celebration of the Mass, which
no one attended.

Michael had declined prestigious posts in the
West which could have made him an international
theologian. Like the deprived poor around him, he
and his two companions had chosen to be victims of
their commitment to obscurity. He maintained that
Christ, the Word, the *logos* revealed himself through
dia-logue, as the 'moral passover' deepened. The
language and sentences he used were poetic. The
Buddhist culture had refined his theology into an art
form so that Michael's words at times seemed to pro-
ceed from the eternal Word held in the silence of God.
Authentic theology is always beautiful. The spirit of
joy came upon us as we parted. His final sentences
still sparkle like jewels in my mind:

> I thought that my voyage had come to its end
> at the last limit of my power; that the path
> before me was closed; that provisions were
> exhausted and the time come to take shelter
> in silent obscurity. But I find that Thy will,

O God, knows no end in me. And when old
words die out on the tongue, new melodies
break forth from the heart; and where the
old tracks are lost, a new country is revealed
with all its wonders.[3]

Liminality and conversion

I came home converted like the prodigal son of Luke
15, to a deeper appreciation of the grace of God who,
like a Father, seeks to enfold the whole world in his
embrace. I came home converted like Peter in Acts 10
to an enlarged vision of the mission of God. The transforming of a person's perspective is no easy matter,
for such transitions are fraught with resistance and
danger. We are transformed by the renewing of our
minds, but our minds are trapped by subconscious
perspectives (Rom. 12.2).

Michael Polanyi investigates this resistance to the
new in the realms of art and science. He argues that
seeing and hearing in a new way will only take place
when a person is persuaded to abandon the familiar
world-view and live wholeheartedly in a new one. This
happens when the former interpretive framework
crumbles or is destroyed by a self-critical act. Polanyi
uses the language of repentance, conversion and worship to describe this process just as I am using 'edge
of Pentecost' to describe liminality. Radical change
always involves a traumatic breaking process because
'our reason is slave to our passions'. Communication
at this subconscious level is not a rational or technical problem; it is an ethical one, since our very
identity is threatened. This is why in our exploration
of preacher's theology I argued that the Holy Spirit
alone enables a deep penetration of the gospel.

Returning home

When I cycled through the gates of the college at the start of the new term I knew everything had changed. The ride from Moss Side via Manchester University, up the Oxford Road, through Rusholme to the leafy location of the College near Platt Fields takes you through several worlds. Moss Side had been part of my life from the beginning, likewise the University and College but I remained detached from the vibrant colourful Asian world of Rusholme. Now I wanted to embrace it. My sabbatical had removed blinkers. Anticipating my teaching commitments I had been wondering how I could apply what I had learnt in the far country to the situation here.

I encountered an immediate difficulty in communicating with some of the staff. They were unable to appreciate the profound change which had taken place in me. They listened to my 'words' but failed to 'hear' what I was saying. It was like trying to describe music to someone who is deaf. They had not been where I had been. Support, however, was to come from an unexpected quarter.

In the autumn term of 1987 a group of overseas theological educators under the auspices of what was then the British Council of Churches visited a number of theological establishments in Britain.[4] Their conclusions are illuminating:

- Students seem more concerned with questions like 'how can I defend my position?' rather than 'how can I learn from a different perspective?'

- There is a lack of awareness that Britain is a multicultural and multifaith society.

- Mission is seen as a separate subject on the curriculum rather than a singular, all-pervasive perspective of gospel and life.

- The British Churches are more concerned to keep the old Britain alive rather than address the contemporary situation.

Needless to say, when their report hit the college it was not well received. I decided I could no longer continue as a college tutor. If liberation and solidarity were to become the foundational norms, then theology had to be done in the context of the local church and community.

A few years later I was a member of a small working party set up to consider the future of ministerial formation. Most of us had a global perspective. Our report was trashed by the colleges and labelled a 'dreamers' report'. The difficulty in communicating a global perspective had not gone away. If every Christian is to be a theologian how are we to bring together the global community, the specialist theological community and the local church, which in theory should be the primary theological community?

At a motorway service station

Before we venture into part three of our journey, let's stop at a service station and see what's on the menu:

- Preacher's theology centring on Jesus Christ, the Word made flesh.

- Charismatic theology springing from an experience of the Holy Spirit.

- Global theology witnessing to God the universal Father.

This trinitarian pattern is fine as far as it goes but does it have universal application? How convenient it would be to throw these theologies in a pot, stir them up, pop them in the oven and produce one all-purpose meal: a sort of McDonald's theological cheeseburger. Sadly such a culinary experiment does not work.

My theology was the product of where I had been and what God had said and done in a number of different contexts. It also focused on liminal moments of revelation. You may not have travelled far or encountered traumatic transitions, but this does not invalidate your own theological journey; it simply makes it different from mine. Are you being transformed? Are you able to trace God's story within your own? Can you articulate it? These are key questions for us all.

Theology, by its very nature, is diverse. Any attempt to produce one theology for all constricts and constrains. As Graham, Walton and Ward conclude 'theology is culturally, temporally and spatially located . . . the gospel cannot exist independent of particular embodied expressions'.[5] This is another way of saying there is no single theological package and that 'fast-food' versions are not on the menu. They seriously damage your health.

It is not surprising, therefore, that Barth, after a lifetime of theological study, laughed at his own efforts (see above, p. 50) and wanted to start all over again from a different point. At best we can only set up theological markers on our journey. There is a grand narrative, but it remains hidden in God. Like the disciples after the feeding of the 5,000, those of us who engage in theology can only gather up the scraps left over from the feast.

We are therefore invited to collect up the fragments joyfully, rejoice in the miracle of revelation and celebrate the mystery. The focus of celebration is the meal of Holy Communion where the separate pieces are brought together to become one. In the Eucharist we also anticipate the riches of our inheritance. In the breaking of bread we await Pentecost.

THEOLOGICAL EXPLORATION

- How is your church engaging in justice issues? What are you doing?

- Share any experience you have had of being in a 'far country'. How has it changed your perspectives?

- Reflect on your theological journey thus far. Do you think of your theology as: (i) a package, (ii) a set of markers on a journey, (iii) a story, (iv) an application of the creeds, (v) a programme, (vi) other ways? Can you explain?

Question for the next chapter

How do transitions affect us?

Part 3
What is the Spirit saying?

8

Transitions and Transformation

In this third part I want to encourage you to listen to what God's Spirit is saying to us today. I have already reflected upon a number of liminal transitions within my own theological and spiritual journey. There are more to come in this concluding part, both personal and social. Our Western culture, the Church and the planet are all poised on the edge of dangerous boundaries. Nevertheless, Ezekiel's vision, with which this book began, persuades me that we stand on a threshold of hope; the dawn of a new Pentecost.

This chapter and part of the next are personal, telling how the Spirit has led me through the more recent transitional periods of my life. The next two chapters explore what standing on the edge of Pentecost means; Chapter 9 looks at revelation and brokenness, Chapter 10 at illumination and blessing. Chapter 11 asks: 'What is the Spirit saying to the Churches?' The final chapter considers the future of the planet and our responsibility for the next generation.

Agape and eros

In August 1982, just a few weeks before we left Exeter, my mother died of lung cancer. My father was devastated. He had lovingly tended her at home. At the very time when he needed us most we moved 240 miles away to Manchester.

The death of one parent and the abandonment of the other invariably releases a flood of emotion. It affected us all as a family. My journal contains long entries, psycho-dynamic diagrams and prayers. I was travelling the bereavement path and trying to make sense of the unresolved Freudian stuff of earlier years. This got me thinking about the age-old tension between *agape* and *eros* so apparent in the life of Augustine, though not satisfactorily resolved by his theology.

Eros, according to C.S. Lewis, is the Greek word for 'love' which the New Testament writers rejected because of its association with sexual desire and pagan worship. Pope Benedict XVI's first encyclical, entitled *Deus Caritas Est*, attempts to counter the criticism that Christianity destroys *eros*. Unfortunately, the encyclical still fails to appreciate the positive contribution of sexuality and sensuality. Both C.S. Lewis and Pope Benedict remain trapped within a masculine theology that sidelines the experience of women. Feminist and liberation theologies demand that the Church listens to the voices it has marginalized.

I had hitherto drawn from a theological tradition in which the key players were men. They wrote in conceptual language, thought of revelation as something coming from beyond and maintained ecclesiastical control of doctrine. The feminist theologian and writer Mary Grey helped me see how, alongside the dominant *logos* theology of objectivity and rationality, there is also a feminine theology of s*ophia* or wisdom which is subjective and relational.[1] The male theological tradition asserts truth in statements and formula like my Richmond creed. This often leads to confrontation, division, reductionism and even crusade. The more hidden female stream is concerned with integrating 'body' and 'spirit', and finds 'truth' through the experience of 'connected knowing'. Revelation, according to Rosemary Ruether, has more to do with the quest for full humanity than it does with 'God-talk'.

How we interpret the Old Testament Song of Songs, which almost failed to be included in Scripture, tells us a lot about ourselves and the Church. Most Catholic and Protestant theologies spiritualize away its sensuality and eroticism. This should not surprise us, given that the book uses fantasy and playful intimacy to subvert sterile theology. Sadly, many Christians avoid the 'garden of delights' and prefer to live in the shadow of Eden, concealing their nakedness because they are ashamed. Today we wear face masks instead of fig leaves to hide our vulnerability. It seems strange that we, who believe in the incarnation and the cross, shy away from the physical. I often wonder where the risen Christ got his white robes from after leaving the grave cloths behind. Maybe it is too daring for artists to paint a risen Christ who is naked! I happen to believe in the resurrection of the body not the resurrection of the contents of wardrobes.

The Church seems to have a polluted view of sexuality, treating it as a wild beast by shutting it up in a cage. Sexual passion can certainly be strong, but it is not as powerful as fear or as strong as death. Locking up sexuality can, for some, inflame its ability to wreak terrible destruction through other means. In the first flush of a charismatic experience one is tempted to think that erotic desire has been swallowed up in *agape* and that sin, like some cancers, has been plucked out. Sin always has secondaries, for holiness is not a state of arrival but a journey of becoming. The issue is not so much about being sinless but rather of being self-aware and human.

The journey of becoming

During my spell in Sri Lanka I spent a week in a Buddhist retreat centre at Nilambe. Situated in mountains above the tea estates, you stand on top of the world. I went to see Paprushka, a Dane who lived in a hut nearby. He was 84, eccentric and full of laughter. I could not prevent myself from smiling the whole time I was with him. He related the familiar parable of the sower and asked why the seed did not grow. I gave all the standard answers. Like a playful child he bounced up and down. 'Wrong! Wrong! Wrong! You do not know your own Christian gospel; you learned men never do. It is because there is no humour in the soil.' His podgy flesh rippled with glee. This was my introduction to a Buddhist retreat.

I was the only Christian. Godwin Sararathene was the spiritual director. The food was dreadful – a lot of chewing was required. Even the dog eating the left-overs was sick. We rose from our concrete slabs each morning at 4.40 a.m. to sit in silence in the unadorned hall until 7.30; again from 10.30 a.m. to noon, then from 4.00 p.m. to 6.00 p.m. and finally from 7.30 to 8.30 p.m. During the first two days I wanted to escape from what felt like imprisonment. Eventually I learned to breathe, still my agitated body, my mind and then my spirit. I never had any fear that something evil would enter me in the 'blissful void'. Christ was before me, around me and within me. Eventually, through combinations of breathing, *glossalalia* and the Jesus Prayer, I seemed to move beyond space and time. My memories are of inner expansiveness, star-filled heavens at night, dancing fireflies, deep inner peace and bedbugs.

I had a personal interview with Godwin. He listened in silence as I drowned him in a torrent of words. When after an hour they ceased he still held his silence. Finally he spoke. 'Be gentle with yourself.' That was all. The interview was over, but it was enough to move my spiritual and theological journey on and prepare me for my meeting with Father Mike a few weeks later.

I was 'trying too hard'; living by law and not by grace. Moreover, my preoccupation with 'self' had made life difficult for those close to me. During those months away my thoughts and prayers turned increasingly to Christine and the children back in Manchester. In being hard on myself, I had been hard and neglectful of them. In 'beating myself up' I was shutting down my creative side where potentiality and chaos, *agape* and *eros* dwelt together in the darkness. I had forgotten that inner darkness could become 'friendly darkness' because God had redeemed it. Through my exposure to fear in war-torn Sri Lanka I had contemplated my own death and discovered that love is stronger than death. It is our flawed nature that keeps us in touch with our humanity and enables us to identify deeply with the brokenness of others. Although great inequality of gifts, power and possessions exist between persons, there is no inequality with respect to sin. We have all fallen short. Being human is living with the mess.

Poetic theology

I returned to Manchester laden with experiences from the far country. I returned more aware of Christine, Martin, Matthew and Joanne who in different ways were making their own journeys of discovery. They had released me because they loved me. My father was delighted to hear about my travels. My stories gave him a new focus of interest.

Although God is present in places of pain and marginalization, I had come to see that the universe also belongs to the dancer. 'Cold theology' freezes the dance. Calvinism restricts creativity by trapping sexuality within the strait-jacket of the Law. *Eros,* chaos and mess are raw materials awaiting the transforming presence of the Spirit. That creative Spirit now bubbled in me. I had crossed a liminal threshold. It was as if the nervous circuits in my brain had been altered; as if I'd been rewired. No longer in the pupa stage, I was ready to fly like a butterfly.

Don Cupitt suggests that St Augustine banished the idea of 'poetic theology' because he had identified it with *eros* and the old myths.[2] What was gushing up in me was something I too had banished in favour of creeds and scientific theology. When creeds police language, something dies. Sticking with the rational and scientific empties language of its symbolic significance. All fundamentalisms kill imagination.

Father Mike had shown me how true theology is beautiful. Music had always spoken to my soul. Now poetry started to flow. Contemplating the turn of the seasons after an early morning walk in Alexandra Park, Manchester, I penned:

The crisp chill air, red berries like drops of
blood upon the trees,
And dew-like tears tell me I have come alive
For I did not know till now
That I was dead.

The rustling leaves murmur and dance in
the desolate hedge.
Then shines the sun, shimmering
through bare branches.
The fisherman swings his hopeful line
Tossing it to break the surface
Of the silent water.

When nature dies the earth turns on its axis
away from light.
There was a shadow part of me, sealed off
Entombed in the place of death
Brimming with possibilities
Beyond my dreams.

Red berries like drops of blood and tears on
a frosty morning
Announce that life when lived
Is living now.

Revelling in the fact that I had a Sunday without
church commitments, and could therefore spend the
whole day with Christine and the children walking in
the Peak District I wrote:

The distant bell on a still Sunday morning
Sounds out to call the religious remnants.
In ecclesial clumps, they trudge along
In faithful devotion on empty pavements.

We drive off now, for the slumbering city
Spews out its shoppers in bustling haste

We are away to the whispering trees
  The rain sodden hills and wilderness waste.

Where shall I go?

I had hoped to return to Sri Lanka, taking a group
of students with me, and stay with Father Mike. It
was not to be. On the evening of 10 November 1987
at about 7.30 p.m., while pronouncing the benedic-
tion at the end of a celebration of the Mass, Michael
Rodrigo was shot through the head by an unknown
assassin. He died instantly. His blood filled the chalice
they had used. The news was brought to me as I sat in
the chapel following our own college Communion. I
went home and wrote:

Where shall I go from here, O Father Mike?
  Your face, your voice, recaptured in your
    verse.
All the simplicity of a saint caught in
    childlike sketches.
  I hear your cry for justice.
  I feel your joy.
You awoke in me a forgotten dream,
Lost in a vocation cracked and tarnished.

Where shall I go from here, O Father Mike?
  Do I follow you to some concrete waste?
An abandoned place where the
    dispossessed struggle for meaning?
  I hear their cry for justice.
  I feel your pain.
Your brain splashed by an assassin's gun,
The wine and blood mingled in a chalice.

Where do the poor go now, O Father Mike?
  For now bereft, they've lost their champion.
The night grows darker and the flickering
    candle is extinguished.
  The poor have lost their star,
  I feel their loss.
O sad and defiled 'good wishes' house,
  Who will go now to that desolate place?

The death of Father Mike sealed my decision to leave college. I had to return to 'normal' ministry; but where? I felt I was being led to work with the urban poor. The Church instead sent me to the rich boom town of Reading in the royal county of Berkshire.

Not the job I wanted

I raised objections. I kept haranguing God in my prayers: 'What are you doing sending me to minister amongst the rich when I am ready to work alongside the poor?' Of course, I was characterizing notions of rich and poor, for Reading, like most places, had its share of the marginalized. Much to my dismay I discovered not only that I had oversight of four vast Victorian Methodist edifices in the town centre but found we needed a million pounds to repair them. This was not the job I wanted.

Amazing though it may seem, our eight years in Reading turned out to be the happiest yet. So began a ministry of creativity, consolidation and innovation with a vibrant staff team and a kaleidoscope of colourful challenges. Although God is dangerous, in Reading I also found God to be playful. He laughs at our attempts to box him up in religion, creeds and buildings.

It was strange how the death of Father Mike released freedom and fulfilment in me. Words of Thomas Merton summed up what I was feeling:

> For the world and time are the dance of the Lord in emptiness ... and no despair of ours can alter the reality of things, or stain the joy of the cosmic dance which is always there. Indeed, we are in the midst of it, and it is in the midst of us, for it beats in our very blood, whether we want it to or not.[3]

Creativity was at last allowed free expression. I began painting watercolour seascapes. I had seldom picked up a paint brush since school days because I had been told, 'You are no good at art because you can't stay within the lines.' It was an astonishing comment from an art teacher.

Two important legacies of my ministry in Reading are personally significant. The church rebuilding scheme is not one of them, though it swallowed up inordinate amounts of time and effort. The first was the establishing of the Women's Centre, a project alongside the poor. You can read about it in *Beyond the Box*.[4] The second was the creation of a painting workshop for those who thought they were not artistic but then discovered they had more talent than they hitherto imagined.

Reading was a place of consolidation and growth in faith. It was also the time when our first grandchild, Ben, was born. My theology had come together; so had Christine and I in a happiness of fulfilment. There is, however, a downside to everything. In such a well-matched situation one can easily settle down and be comfortable.

New horizons

> My insight once so sharp and keen
>> Is dulled and soiled where once had been
> Idealism, vibrancy and faith,
>> God's risk adventure now played safe.
> For middle age and middle class
>> Has made me keen to hold on fast
> To comfort, status, transient toys,
>> The collected idols my life enjoys.

We had hoped to stay in Reading until 2005, my year of retirement, but in 1998 I was appointed Chair of the Southampton Methodist District. The Methodist Church in Britain is carved up into 32 Districts, each subdivided into circuits. This District, with 15,000 church members, was a large one stretching along the south coast from Weymouth to Rustington (including the Isle of Wight) and bounded in the north by the M4. It swallowed up several counties and Anglican dioceses. The Chair is the Methodist equivalent of a diocesan Bishop. Originally Methodist 'Chairmen' were District Evangelists set free from local pastoral responsibility. I had a brilliant staff team and Marilyn Pack was an exceptional secretary. I took to the job like a duck to water. There was also an added delight because Sam, our second grandchild, was born. The final verse of the above poem written in Manchester had come true; or so I thought:

> I once dreamed there would come a time
>> When God's true moment would meet mine
> And I would know that what had been
>> Was preparation for the scene.

One's theological journey is never smooth. Apocalyptic events were to awaken us all from our comfortable slumbers.

THEOLOGICAL EXPLORATION

- How has the Church helped or hindered your approach to issues of sexuality?

- How do you personally cope with change?

- At the end of Chapter 4, I suggested you write your own statement of faith (creed). Have a go at trying to express some aspect of your faith in a poem. You may want to share it with the group next time.

Question for the next chapter

Are we living in apocalyptic times?

9

Apocalypse Now

One reason for accepting the Reading appointment was to be near my father. The geographical distance between Manchester and Somerset had become a problem, particularly during his bouts of illness. When we told him we were moving to Reading he was pleased but then added: 'I will never see you in Reading. I will be gone by then.' He was right. He died six months before we moved.

The Greek word *apocalypse* means 'revelation'. It was only after my father died that I recalled his words. What prompted him to say this? What did he see? The word 'apocalypse' goes beyond premonition or a flash of insight. Apocalypse refers to a pulling back of the cosmic curtain to give us a peep into God's 'grand narrative'. Apocalypse is a form of prophecy. It reveals God's 'news' behind the media 'news'. Since human beings 'cannot bear very much reality'[1] we create worlds of 'virtual reality', where evil is masked, violence glamorized, illusions embraced, terror airbrushed out, truth fantasized and death disguised. Jesus said there was nothing hidden which would not one day be revealed (Lk. 12.2).

The destruction of Disneyland

It was 11 September 2001 and I was visiting a church member in a local hospital. The television was on. I thought they were showing an American disaster movie as fire billowed out of one of the Twin Towers. But this was not fantasy. This was reality.

As news started to filter through, a teacher in a primary school in America (so I heard later) tried to explain to her class what was happening. One of the children asked, 'Are they bombing Disneyland?' She thought about it and concluded that the child's question had prophetically stated the truth behind 9/11. Shaped by malign structures, ruled by powerful economic magnates, conditioned by image manipulators skilled in creating illusion, it is not easy to distinguish between 'virtual reality' and 'true reality'. 9/11 blew away our Disneyland world of virtual reality.

Just before the attack, Chalmers Johnson, another American, had written:

> The innocent in the rich world in the 21st century are going to harvest unexpected blowback disasters from the imperious escapades of recent decades. Although most Americans may be largely ignorant of what was and still is being done in their name, they are likely to pay a steep price individually and collectively for their nation's continual effort to dominate the global scene.[2]

Rowan Williams said we tasted for a brief moment the experience of the majority of people on our planet who live each day under the threat of random death.

In his book *Apocalypse Now*, Duncan Forester, speaking of 'furious religion', records his reaction when he saw the first pictures of the burning towers. Avoiding the theological tomes on the book-shelf he took down the Bible, opened it at Mark 13, read of the destruction of another great building and wondered if apocalyptic thinking had come back with a vengeance.

Apocalyptic thinking is back

Apocalyptic theology went out of fashion in Britain after the religious wars of the seventeenth century, to be replaced by rational 'Enlightenment' faith (pages 52–3). Hot theology became cool theology.

The attacks of 9/11 have placed apocalyptic theology back on the table. Enlightened 'liberal' theology is being driven from the menu by a growing appetite for fast-food fundamentalism: that closed system of thought which gives a person passion and certainty. Fundamentalism can position itself at any point of the theological, religious or political spectrum. It seeks to triumph over alternative views. In our contemporary twilight zone of clashing ideologies the deep corruption of the human mind and will is again being revealed.

In a sermon preached one week after 9/11, I returned to the tough tale of Cain and Abel:

> We no longer live in the land of Eden. The age of innocence has passed. We now inhabit a violent world of inequalities. Why does God prefer Abel's gift to Cain's? It seems so unfair until you do a bit of background work. The Hebrew word for Cain means 'bring forth'. Cain, the firstborn son, inherited productive land. The Hebrew for Abel means 'nothing'

or 'vapour'. The two sons did not start equal. Cain had everything; Abel had nothing and was forced to become a wandering nomad. When they brought their gifts, God took Abel's side. This provoked explosive anger in Cain. His countenance fell and instead of looking to God he became a dangerous animal and murdered his brother. 'Where is your brother?' asks God. Denying all responsibility for others Cain himself is cast into the role of a fugitive living in fear.

9/11 tells me I have poverty-stricken brothers and sisters in the Sudan, in Mozambique, Zimbabwe, Darfur, Iraq and Saudi Arabia. It awakens me to the reality of global injustice. The Genesis story tells me that if the pride or achievement of a rich powerful nation like the United States is damaged, as Cain's was, that nation must beware lest it launch a pre-emptive strike. Such action will not only be unjust but will spawn further fear and violence. If the US or Britain launch an attack against Iraq we ourselves will come under the wrath of God.

Rational ideas of 'just war' and 'just deterrence' have now become obsolete; the replacement of Trident is an aberration. Future wars will be civil wars, communal clashes between ideological groups. Terrorism is cyclical and repetitive. It will not go away. Philip Jenkins, in his chilling book *The Next Christendom*, suggests that the expansion of Christianity and Islam across countries and within countries will precipitate fanatical religious conflicts and create more ecological disasters. He thinks we stand on the threshold of 'the next crusade' and presents us with a very bleak future in which Christians and Muslims blunder into new conflicts.

Apocalyptic theology

Since 9/11 other apocalyptic storm clouds have rolled over the horizon. We have witnessed 7/7, the tsunami, gun violence, floods and the growing consequences of climate change. The biblical prelude to the flood tells how God looked upon the earth and was overcome with grief (Gen. 6.6). The words 'the earth was corrupt in God's sight, and the earth was filled with violence' (v.11) continue to toll like a funeral bell. Reminiscent of Noah's flood, the primal waters of chaos are starting to engulf the planet. I spoke of this in the Methodist Conference of 2006:

> The four horsemen of the apocalypse are already galloping across our planet leaving trails of destruction in their wake. The white horse of imperialism – some would say American globalization; the fiery red horse of military invasion and terrorist atrocity; the black horse of plague, famine and natural disaster; and finally the pale horse of death – death from carbon emissions which blot out the sun.

Is apocalypse all about brokenness, doom and gloom? Apocalyptic theology confronts despair and flight into a 'Big Brother House' of virtual reality.

Christian apocalypse challenges the strident claims of the demonic principalities and powers by drawing attention to the Lamb slaughtered from the foundation of the world. This vulnerable victorious figure now lives to receive power, wealth, wisdom, might, honour, glory and blessing because he has absorbed into himself all the rage, fear and violence that has ever existed or will exist (Rev. 5.6–14). Apocalyptic theology does not call Christians to fight but rather invites them to worship the trinitarian God who is Alpha and Omega, the beginning and the end. The focal point of history is not 9/11, terrible though it was. The world was changed many years before when a carpenter was slain on Skull Hill. Apocalyptic theology is a theology of hope for hard times. It signals the presence of the Holy One and announces an outpouring of the Spirit.

Thousands of years ago another tower was smashed down in the land of Shinar. It is tempting for us in Britain to live fearfully amongst the desolate ruins of fragmented Babel towers and forget that God is calling us to live in the reversal of that curse. Although the journey from Babel to Pentecost is a long one in the Bible, it is a short one for us. The attacks of 9/11 and subsequent apocalyptic events are blowing away our illusions and drawing us to the edge. The choice is virtual reality or Pentecost: 'I will pour out my spirit on all flesh; your sons and your daughters shall prophesy, your old men shall dream dreams' (Joel 2.28).

Dreams in the night

It is 29 June 2004. I am at the Methodist Conference in Loughborough puzzling over a dream I had a few nights before:

> I saw myself sitting beneath a huge tree whose branches stretched to protect me from a terrible storm. I looked at peace. The tree had deep roots which went down forever. The tree transformed itself into a fig tree. A voice said, 'Honour me and I will honour you.'

I had again been pressed by several people to allow my name to be considered for President. I hesitated: I am due to retire in 2006 – my health is uncertain – I am too old and flawed for such demands – the Church appoints sensible people, not those who have strange dreams in the night. A friend said, 'If you do not let your name go forward will you have regrets in the future?' Not knowing what to do, I placed myself in the hands of Conference. That night I dreamt again:

> I was looking in terror across a vast wilderness. In all directions I saw the scattered bones of countless human skeletons. An insistent voice kept repeating, 'Can these bones live?' I awoke with phrases in my head, grabbed some paper and scribbled: The Spirit in the Trinity blowing through the world, reshaping the Church, renewing individuals. Speak the Word.

The next day it was announced that I had been elected President of the Methodist Conference for the year September 2005 to 2006.

Bewildered and battered

When I heard this I bent over and wept. Christine was similarly overcome. It was unexpected and baffling.

For the rest of Conference we went around in a daze. I now understood the significance of my dream about the 'valley of dry bones'. God had given me the message, which is the theme of this book. I must 'honour God' by speaking about the Holy Spirit who is about to renew the Church and restore confidence through his Word. If the Methodist people are to be part of this then we must learn quickly how to talk of God with sense and conviction. I was to encourage every Methodist to be a theologian (the meaning of sitting under a fig tree).

When I returned home, hard questions hit me. Was I losing touch with reality and living in a world of dreams? Had the Church made a dreadful mistake? Would my Presidency bring disaster upon the Church? Was I about to lead the Church into a fantasy land of false hope? For months I waded through the swamp of denial, bewilderment and fear. Very few people knew of this. I hid behind a mask and got on with the job of being Chair, writing a book and preparing for a Presidency which I felt I would never take up.

My health was the immediate concern. Within weeks of returning from Conference I saw a consultant at Winchester Hospital. While waiting for an investigation I happened to look at the bookmark accidentally left in the novel I was reading. On it was a text:

> 'I know the plans I have for you,' declares the Lord, 'plans to prosper you and not harm you, plans to give you hope and a future. Then you will call upon me, and I will listen to you. You will seek me and find me when you seek me with all your heart' (Jer. 29.11f.).

I expected good news from the consultant but instead had to live with uncertainty. The burden hung over us for months until I had the 'all clear'.

Secondly, there were anxieties within our family which kept us awake night after night. While on holiday in Cornwall we were faced with the possibility that Chris had cancer. I recall stopping our car in the middle of Dartmoor; my mind in turmoil. We read 2 Corinthians 4.1–10. Chris looked radiant. I felt crushed. She wrote the text on a piece of paper, I placed it in a polythene bag and hid it under a stone. I suspect it is still there:

> A blanket of cloud hung over the moor but the sun was shining in the far distance. Would the clouds part and bathe us in the sun? On my journey home from Winchester Hospital after my own cancer scare months before, a rainbow appeared giving me hope. As we sat in silence the clouds at last slowly began to roll away. The rich colours of the gorse and heather sparkled. We lay on our backs looking up at the blue dome of the sky.

Liminality

Just in case you still stumble over the word 'liminality' which crops up in this final part, can I remind you of the transition of caterpillar to butterfly. 'Liminality', as I am using it, applies to the pupa stage. It is a dangerous 'on the edge' of something moment in a process of transformation.

Nanette Stahl, in her book *Law and Liminality in the Bible*, examines some incidents of liminality.

She reflects on Jacob's struggle with the angel at the Jabbok ford (Gen. 32.22f.):

> This incident deals with a border, or threshold, in the more literal sense. At the very moment when Jacob is about to enter the land and claim his birthright, an attempt is made to hinder, if not actually bar him from crossing over. The struggle threatens to physically prevent the liminal moment from taking place . . . It is as if, at the last minute, God has doubts over the relationship into which he is about to enter . . . Only midway in the struggle does Jacob's sheer force of will tilt the balance in his favour.[3]

My overriding struggle was with fear. It permeated everything; fear of losing a loved one, fear that illness would prevent me from functioning, fear that I would have to function without finding a way out, fear of letting everyone down, fear of unworthiness, the fear of fear. It felt as if forces were arrayed against us, trying to drown us in an abyss.

It took more than nine months from my nomination for the darkness to completely lift and for the pupa stage to be left behind. We felt ourselves swept up on a tide of prayer. Some people had obviously been praying all the time for there had been flashes of light during the gloom. In my journal entry on 7 February 2005 I record how I was praying in my study. A robin started to sing so loudly that I stopped, listened and looked from the window. I wrote (with apologies to Thomas Hardy):

> I watched a robin sing and wondered why?
> Celebration, anticipation,

A glimpse of blue across the wintry sky?
I worry and fear what tomorrow may
    bring,
    Revelation, destruction,
    Storms of shame, a tainted offering?
That little bird is wiser far than I,
    Watching, waiting,
    Sensing a loving God in its hopeful cry.

Another significant revelation took place in one of the small chapels of our District on 14 September 2004. At the end of a tedious business meeting someone in the group asked if they could pray for me. They knew nothing of our struggles. I was asked to kneel. The ten people present gathered round, placed their hands on my head and prayed. This had seldom happened since my ordination. One of the members phoned afterwards to say God had spoken to her about me as they prayed. 'God is saying to you, I will if you will. Everything in your past life is preparing you for this coming time.' I had a flashback of those incidents recorded in Chapters 2 and 3 when I was told 'One day you will be President of the Conference.'

At last I was ready to take up the office and deliver the message God had given me. Among the many letters I received there was one from a retired minister who enclosed the following:

When I was a lad I was no fool,
    I was sent by my parents to the Sunday
        School.
I collected money for the JMA
    And did my bit on Anniversary Day.
I read my poems with such eloquence
    That now I'm the President of the
        Conference.

After many verses of this 'take-off' of Gilbert and Sullivan it concludes:

> Now Methodists all, whoever you may be
>> If you want to rise in the hierarchy,
> It doesn't matter if your faith is poor,
>> Your Bible gone and your voice is sore,
> Just go to all the meetings and the church events
>> And they'll make you the President of the Conference.

It was full of inaccuracies as I had always done my best to avoid church meetings, but it made me laugh. There would now be meetings of a different kind, providing unique opportunities to honour God and speak of his renewing word and the Spirit.

THEOLOGICAL EXPLORATION

- How has 9/11 or subsequent apocalyptic events affected you or the people in your area?

- If you feel able, share how you have coped with some traumatic event in your own life or in the life of your family. How has it changed you?

- In this troubled world what are your grounds for confidence and hope.

Question for the next chapter

Are we on the edge of Pentecost?'

10

Pentecost

In the September of my Presidency I wrote an article for the *Methodist Recorder* about Pentecost:

> Jesus, according to Luke 4, announced his mission manifesto. He was to bring good news, release captives, help blind people see, remove oppression and preach the Jubilee year of debt release. Full of the Spirit, he handed this vision on to us with a promise. 'You will receive power when the Holy Spirit has come upon you; and you will be my witnesses in Jerusalem, in all Judea and Samaria, and to the ends of the earth' (Acts 1.8) . . . What stands in the way of our rediscovering the power and presence of the Holy Spirit?[1]

Many Pentecosts

I quoted from the prophet Joel in the last chapter. Peter uses this apocalyptic text to explain to a bewildered crowd the significance of Spirit baptism and speaking in tongues. On the Day of Pentecost the waiting Church received the first instalment (2 Cor.1.22) of its millionaire inheritance, and leapt over a liminal boundary into a mission of transformation. Luke also records a second occasion when the Spirit is downloaded so powerfully that the Church goes into overdrive:

> When they had prayed, the place in which they were gathered together was shaken; and they were all filled with the Holy Spirit and spoke the word of God with boldness. (Acts 4.31)

How are we to interpret this? The apostles have already been filled with the Spirit. Was this a top-up because they leaked? Was this something extra to launch them across a new threshold? Certainly the Acts 10 account of Peter's mission to Cornelius has all the marks of liminality so reminiscent of Jacob's wrestling at Peniel (p. 114). God in a dream invites Peter to eat unclean animals. He refuses. Three men from Cornelius arrive with a message. He is perplexed. The Spirit prompts him. He delays. He struggles to cross the boundary but having done so, a Pentecostal ignition takes place:

> While Peter was still speaking, the Holy Spirit fell upon all who heard the word. The circumcised believers ... were astounded that the gift of the Holy Spirit had been poured out even on the Gentiles, for they heard them speaking in tongues and extolling God. (Acts 10.44f.)

The Pentecost experience is variable, charismatic, transforming and repeatable. It is essential for a breakthrough in mission. Luke, in Acts 4, 'cooks the books' to give us an idealistic picture of the first Christian community in which believers are of one heart and mind, holding everything in common. He next tells stories of discord (Acts 5.1–11) and discrimination (Acts 6.1–6). It seems that the filling of the Spirit is not a permanent condition. The Church needs to be filled with the Spirit again and again because it is leaky through disobedience and because God wishes to take it across new boundaries. The Church's pilgrimage, like yours and mine, goes forward in fits and starts. As Martyn Atkins puts it, 'The Holy Spirit in Acts is less like the oil of charism and more like WD40 – freeing up rather than blessing up.'[2]

Many Pentecosts are necessary. They seal our ecclesiastical inheritance as pledges and first fruits (Eph. 1.13–14) of what is to come. The Church is instructed to keep on being filled (Eph. 5.18–20) because it is both at Pentecost and on the edge of Pentecost. We are not yet in a full relationship with the Spirit. That fullness belongs to the *eschaton* (the end) when God sums up all things in Christ.

Surfing the Spirit

This tension between the now and the not yet suggests fluidity and movement within the Trinity. Thomas Merton sums this up admirably:

> God, who is everywhere, never leaves us. Yet he seems sometimes to be present, sometimes absent . . . He is like the wind that blows where it pleases. You who love him must love him as arriving from where you do not know and as going where you do not know. Your spirit must seek to be as clean and as free as his own Spirit, in order to follow him wherever he goes.[3]

Responding to the Spirit is like surfing. You have to wait in an appropriate place to catch the breaking wave and leap. There are times when the waves of the Spirit have little power and gently lap the shore. There are other occasions when they tower and crash with such force that the surfer risks injury for the ride of a lifetime.

The Pentecost of Acts 2 was only the start of a wild ride as God undid the curse of Babel and drove the geographical centre of the Church from Jerusalem westwards via Antioch to Rome and eastward to Ethiopia and India. The Spirit through the centuries has continued to propel the Church across barriers and boundaries until Jewish Christianity became Hellenistic, Eastern, European and now global.

Today the wind of the Spirit is blowing through the Southern hemisphere, enlivening the poor of Africa, Asia, the Pacific and Latin America. Almost 60 per cent of Christians now live in these regions. In 1900 there were 10 million African Christians; now there are 400 million. It is estimated that by 2050 only about one fifth of the world's three billion Christians will be non-Hispanic whites. The era of Western Christianity is over. The day of Southern Christianity has dawned.

Pentecostalism is transforming the Christian global landscape. Pentecostal churches are largely lay-led, indigenous and fundamentalist. They manifest themselves as movements of liberation and transformation. Of the four historic strands of Christianity, namely Orthodox, Catholic, Protestant and Pentecostal, the latter is in the ascendant.

This growth is also true of the black churches in Britain, many of which are found in our inner cities.

In 1998 there were 214,600 people attending, now there are around 288,000. This is in stark contrast to the bleak statistics of the other churches in Britain.

Statistics, decline and expansion

In the autumn of 2005 the following statistics were published. The percentages indicate changes in attendance between 1998 and 2005:

Pentecostals	+ 34%
Smaller denominations	+ 9%
Orthodox	+ 2%
Independent Churches	- 1%
New Churches	- 8%
Baptists	- 8%
Anglican	- 11%
Methodist	- 24%
Roman Catholic	- 28%
United Reformed	- 43%

I was with the leaders of Churches Together in England when these figures appeared. Although there was a hint of panic from one member the rest of us were mildly optimistic. The disastrous nosedive of 1990, when over a million people stopped attending church, had not continued. The following day I received an email from the secretary of Churches Together which contained a comment from Grace Davie, Professor of Sociology and Director for European Studies at Exeter University:

> I have considerable misgivings about projections which examine past and current attendance or membership and use them to predict the future. This kind of forecast depends on the notions that all other things

are equal. Never in my professional life have I known a time when this is less likely to be the case.

One month later I posed a question to the leaders of the Methodist Church. 'What is the Spirit saying to us?' I suggested an answer to the astonished gathering. 'We are on the edge of Pentecost.'

The word 'decline' has seeped into the soul of our Church. Our conversations are about reduction, downsizing, and cut-backs. This has sapped our confidence, drained our energy, and created a feeling of 'What's the point?' We must banish the word 'decline' from our vocabulary. God is reshaping the Church. Thirty years ago sociologists were writing about an irreversible secularization. Today many are commenting on the return of religion. The real casualty of decline is not falling numbers but what it has done to people's imagination.

Talk of cuts, rationalization and a reducing Church also produces resistance. Dogged perseverance replaces faith; resignation becomes the substitute for hope. We end up with empty words and dead symbols. As Bono of U2 remarked 'religion is what is left when the Spirit leaves the building'. Our prophecies of decline have become self-fulfilling. I believe we are on the edge of Pentecost. I do not mean Pentecostalism nor do I mean 're-vival'. We stand on the threshold of renewal. We must plan for expansion!

To ensure that the Methodist leaders would not immediately certify me, I invited discussion and comment. Was this prophecy or delusion? The feedback was more positive than I had anticipated. A few questioned whether Pentecost was the right word. Should it be re-formation? One person suggested we might still be in the ruins of Babel, another that I was misguided. Some felt we were close to Pentecost. One member even suggested Pentecost had arrived.

So the 'edge of Pentecost' sound bite was born. Three months later I was to experience Pentecost at first hand when Christine and I visited the Methodist Church in Cuba.

A Cuban experience

'If a person wants to discover Methodism,' said I, preaching through an interpreter to a congregation of nearly a thousand people in Havana, 'then Methodists in Britain must come to Cuba.' Applause broke out. 'We have come to Cuba and discovered that God is here in power and grace; that Pentecost is here.' This provoked thunderous applause and shouts of 'Hallelujah!' as members of the congregation rose to their feet. I had hardly begun my sermon.

In 1960, following the revolution, there were very few ministers left in Cuba. Church membership had dwindled to less than a thousand. Bishop Ricardo Pereira Diaz told us how in the 1970s and 80s his church began to fast and pray. In 1987 membership had grown to 8,000. Now there are over 20,000 members with more than 30,000 people attending worship. In the last few years they have planted 700 mission churches, 1,040 house churches and thousands of cells.

'What is the secret?' I asked. The following ingredients arose from our discussion: (a) prayer and fasting, (b) preaching about the Holy Spirit, (c) every Christian required to speak of what they have seen and heard, (d) every church and every pastor must keep planting new churches.

Of course, sociological and political factors are at work. Since 1959, when the US influence was driven out, Christians have not been allowed to erect church buildings and consequently have to use their homes as 'house churches'. One room gets enlarged, a minister is appointed to lead this 'mission church'. At the same time other cells are planted in other homes which may also develop into 'mission churches'. One 'mission church', which a chairman of the District looked after, had planted 70 'house churches'.

There is a strong 'command' structure, as one would expect in a country ruled by a dictator. Ministers willingly place themselves under the authority of the bishop who sends them to plant churches. There is no shortage of applicants for the ordained ministry, though these must first demonstrate that they have a track record of church planting before they can even be considered for the ordained ministry.

The prohibition against church building is a positive asset to mission, unlike the situation in Britain where the excessive building schemes of the Victorians have given us churches surplus to requirements. The majority of our buildings have become a liability. They demoralize shrinking congregations and freeze mission into maintenance.

The driving out of missionaries and Western influences has led the Methodist Church in Cuba to incorporate the vibrant cultural expressions of the Cuban people in worship. We shall long remember the jazz rhythms of the trumpeters, the syncopated beat of the drums and the galloping pace of the songs and hymns as the congregation waved flags, moved, danced and sang.

Secularity and religion

Christianity should have disappeared in Cuba following the revolution; instead it crossed a liminal threshold, becoming invisible for a while only to emerge with Pentecostal vitality as a 'fresh expression' of church.

Few expected the Church in Britain to survive after the apocalyptic strife of the seventeenth century, yet God raised up Methodism to spread scriptural holiness. Throughout my 40 years of ordained ministry, church leaders and western theologians have predicted the demise of Christianity before the onslaught of secularism. Empty pews, white-haired congregations and warbling choirs again suggest that the Church is finished. The writings of Bishop Spong make excellent sense when viewed from the reasoned perspective of Cambridge or Amsterdam but look distinctly out of place from the perspective of Cuba, Korea or even from some of our inner-city black churches.

The prophets of the 1960s had predicted the ebbing away of religion as the 'God of the gaps' was marginalized by the advance of scientific knowledge (see page 34). It has not happened like this, though some still think it should.

Richard Dawkins, the author of *The God Delusion*, has embraced secular atheism with fundamentalist fervour. He writes beautifully and accurately about science but when he mounts the religious soapbox he resorts to polemical slogans, choosing his ammunition from the worst possible examples of religion. He blames 9/11 on religion, but this is like blaming Hiroshima on science. I like to think that Dawkins' angry blasts are directed not against the small person who comforts herself/himself with what Dawkins regards as the placebo of phoney religion, but rather at the religious institutions of Christianity and Islam.

Having spent a lifetime within the institutional Church I too have seen its bad side and I want to cheer Dawkins on. He at least provokes Christians to think about what they believe; or to put it another way – to become theologians. The institutional Church, however, does not need Dawkins to demolish it; God is doing a more creative job in judging, removing, purging and reshaping it. Dawkins has not grasped that there is good religion and bad religion. Theology pursues good religion which heals rather than harms.

Secularization may still be the name of the game but, like religion, it too is mutating. While a minority are determined to squeeze out religious belief, the majority of people in Britain pursue a less strident form of secularization. This allows for a public expression of religious identity but fixes that expression within basic liberal and democratic ideas of freedom and human rights.

A spiritual vacuum

Some of us who entered the Spirit Zone in the Millennium Dome puzzled over what this empty, egg-like space represented. Was it a secular void? Was it a womb about to give birth to something new? Within the feminization of our society, feelings, signs, symbols, intuition and non-hierarchical relationships are in the ascendant. All these factors came together in a spontaneous expression of religion when Diana, 'the people's princess', died. The public institutions of Church and monarchy were reluctantly forced to accept the people's religion which transformed Diana into the 'queen of hearts' and attributed religious significance to her flawed person. Recent surveys suggest that Britain is becoming a nation of spiritual seekers because people sense 'something' missing from their lives:

> The time is surely coming, says the Lord God, when I will send a famine on the land; not a famine of bread, or a thirst for water, but of hearing the words of the LORD. They shall wander from sea to sea and from north to east; they shall run to and fro, seeking the word of the LORD, but they shall not find it. (Amos 8.11–12)

Religion has been 'de-regulated'. In our British narcissistic culture of consumerism and choice, DIY religion has really caught on, as evidenced in the thirst for Harry Potter and other mixtures of fantasy, magic and darker superstition. People are not turning to the Word of God or to the Church for their answers; rather, as *The Da Vinci Code* excitement demonstrated, many delight in aberrations of the Christian religion. We must beware, however, lest we confuse religion and spirituality. Are football fans, nightclub goers and pill-poppers engaged in a religious activity? Could the emergent spirituality itself be a product of consumerism? Even Christians shop around to find a church which satisfies their need. A consumer economy, even a religious one, is driven by selfishness.

A liminal moment of spirituality

Oliver James has written a book called *Affluenza* in which he contends that the inhabitants of the English-speaking nations are more prone to depression, eating disorders and poor performance than people in less consumer-driven economies.[4] We Westerners are becoming dehumanized as we ourselves become the products of our own consumerism.

The path to Pentecost is one of brokenness in which one's world view is shattered, one's identity lost, one's wants obliterated, one's genuine need revealed. The rapid pace of change is eroding personal identity. Our consumer culture, with its apocalyptic mixture of reality and virtual reality, affluence and affluenza, secularity and spirituality, is precipitating breakdown and fragmentation. There are increasing numbers of people poised on a liminal threshold. Is the Church sufficiently tuned in to contemporary culture to surf on the wave of an emergent spirituality?

A Pentecost breakthrough depends on how closely the Church is identified with these casualties of consumerism and how it responds to them. This is why theology is so important, for it equips us to do this.

THEOLOGICAL EXPLORATION

- What indications are there that people outside the Church are spiritually hungry?

- What do you understand Pentecost to be? Is your church on the edge of Pentecost?

- What prevents you from being 'filled with the Spirit'? What prevents your local church from experiencing Pentecost?

Question for the next chapter

What will the Church in Britain be like in 10 years' time?

11

Churches Old and New

A youth worker persuaded a young girl who attended church regularly to become a member of the Church Council. At the second meeting a long discussion took place about the church having a letter-box. Fed up with the waffle, Amy, with a teenager's sharpness blurted out, 'Why don't you just cut a hole in the door and have done with it?' One of the older women said, 'My, you're being pernickety.' The conversation went on and on, but Amy said no more. She did not understand the meaning of 'pernickety'. When she later discovered how condescending the woman had been she told the youth worker there was no point in going again.[1]

Epitaph for the Church

A huge chasm has opened up between traditional Church and contemporary culture. Unless there are serious attempts to communicate across this cultural boundary, the Church we have inherited will not renew itself. According to the *World Christian Encyclopedia* 53,000 attenders are leaving the Church in Europe and North America every week.[2] Many traditional churches are therefore nearing the end of their shelf-life. William Blake's mournful picture anticipates their epitaph:

I went to the Garden of Love,
And saw what I never had seen
A Chapel was built in the midst,
Where I used to play on the green.

And the gates of this Chapel were shut,
And 'Thou shalt not' writ over the door;
So I turned to the Garden of Love
That so many sweet flowers bore.

And I saw it was filled with graves,
And tombstones where flowers should be;
And priests in black gowns were walking
    their rounds,
And binding with briars my joys and desires.[3]

New life in old churches

When contemplating the bleak statistics of the Church
we should also note that membership of nearly
every institution, from Trade Unions to attendance at
cinemas, is falling. There are still more people turning up for God on Sundays than going to weekend
football matches.

Martyn Percy warns the Churches against panick-
ing over statistics. What has changed is the performance of worshippers who no longer attend regularly.
We should take a more relaxed view since our 'era
continues to be a time of questions, exploration,
wonder and awe'.[4] Grace Davie follows a similar line,
arguing that the traditional churches continue to be
regarded as public utilities for the common good in
which a minority sustain faith on behalf of the wider
population.[5] In apocalyptic moments, like the death
of Princess Diana or 9/11, large numbers of British
people want to make a religious gesture. It is therefore

important for the Churches to recognize and grasp such moments in the life of the nation.

As one time Canon of Salisbury Cathedral and also a member of the Winchester Cathedral Council I had opportunities not only to preach but to be part of the worshipping life of these two great cathedrals. While church attendance is falling overall one cannot fail to be impressed by the large crowds attending the cathedrals on high days and holy days. What is drawing them? While the cynic would speak of nostalgia and folk religion I think it is something to do with sacred and hospitable space. I have already mentioned how most people have an experience of the transcendent but because they lack theological understanding do not associate it with God (page 17). Cathedrals and some historic church buildings have become 'thin places' where time and eternity meet. Some still retain an age-old 'pulling power' and can have a future. However, that future is dependent on the resident congregation who, as sensitive interpreters and theologians, help the outsider explore the mystery. Sadly, few church members are theologically equipped to do this. Some even drive the outsider away, as was the case with Amy at the beginning of this chapter.

Old life in new churches

A seismic cultural shift has taken place, leaving three generations detached from Christian culture and tradition. John Hull, in his theological critique of a report entitled *Mission-shaped Church*, reminds us of a splendid sentence: 'Start with the Church and the mission will probably get lost. Start with mission and it is likely that the Church will be found.'[6] Over the years we have thought of mission as bringing people into church and getting them to accept our beloved liturgical gems. For many outsiders in their young or middle years, coming to church is like visiting another planet. Even small adaptations of existing patterns in worship are often resisted by a congregation trapped under the malign influence of a few older stalwarts. Other accommodations dumb down worship so that neither the lifelong members nor the newcomers are satisfied.

We have reached the end of 'generational' growth whereby the children of Christian parents, through baptism, Sunday school and confirmation, provided for a future membership. 'Conversion' growth is now the only way forward. This means building theological bridges across the cultural divide. Outsiders seeking God are no longer prepared to fight their way through what they regard as a jungle of obsolete ecclesiastical baggage. The theological example of Paul in Acts 17 (page 79) now becomes the primary model. There is plenty of evidence that this approach is starting to pay off. Another report, *Changing Church for a Changing World* contains vibrant examples of 'fresh expressions' of Church.

On my Presidential travels I saw some of these 'fresh expressions' in non-ecclesiastical buildings and 'fresh expressions of worship' in church buildings. Let me give two examples of the former.

In Doncaster, Christine and I participated in worship at the *Junction*. This had once been a pub at the heart of the community. When it become derelict, visionary Christians took it over, repaired and transformed it into a vibrant community centre and church. Most of the people we met would never have crossed the threshold of 'inherited church'. Even though the word 'church' is not used, the essential ingredients of fellowship, the pursuit of justice, evangelism, teaching and Christ-centred worship make it so.

In Kidsgrove, we visited the *Taste and See* coffee bar. They serve excellent cappuccino, provide lunch-time snacks, are holding informal worship and running Alpha Groups for the non-churched. Most of those involved are under 40 years old. Numbers have grown so much that the café is not big enough to contain them. A new church plant has now been added in a local pub. A hundred yards or so down the road from *Taste and See* is a traditional Methodist church. The relationship between the old and the new forms of church is tangled and unclear. If the Church in Britain is to be transformed and renewed there has to be a symbiotic relationship between inherited church and 'fresh expressions'.

A mixed-economy church

John Wesley operated with two models of church. One was the traditional institution focused on ecclesiastical buildings and served by ordained professionals like himself. The other was the 'society' which he thought of as a 'fellowship of believers' led by appointed lay persons. These societies, like some 'fresh expressions', were for outsiders seeking a salvation which they were unable to experience in the Established Church.

In my Conference address, I suggested that Methodists give priority to establishing 'fresh expressions' of church. To achieve this we needed to shift power from the 'local church' to the circuit meeting, thereby making that body the primary resourcing unit for mission:

> Given extra legal authority, the circuit meeting would then be able to close resistant churches, sell off the buildings and use the proceeds to employ and deploy staff in imaginative ways.

This statement was greeted with an enthusiastic cheer. It also touched a raw nerve because I received many letters accusing me of trying to shut small churches. It is not the small churches that hold us back but the nostalgia of members in the larger churches who live with the fantasy of vibrant Sunday schools and tuneful choirs.

The 'fresh expressions' as described in the two reports mentioned (on pages 132–3) are offspring of inherited Church. Like the children of ageing parents they carry the DNA of traditional church with them. While some 'fresh expressions' are very imaginative, others do little more than exchange the organ for the piano, or use PowerPoint™ instead of hymn-books, naively believing this will make a significant difference.

Is our thinking about 'fresh expressions' radical enough? Does it adequately express 'kingdom theology' which is essential if we are in the business of changing the world, rather than just preserving the Church? I therefore propose a third, more adventurous, model. I suggested in my book *Into the Far Country* that 'ecclesial communities' (which could be called 'emerged church') are neither planted, nor are they the product of 'pioneer' ministry but are kingdom communities springing from the soil of some particular need beyond the borders of church. They are fluid, inclusive and transient. Such churches pose difficult theological questions and raise acute issues about oversight. There are very few people with the necessary gifts and training to work with this more radical form of church. 'Emerged churches' as I have defined them require a 'theological consultant' rather than a pioneer minister or leader.

If we focus on mission within a 'mixed economy' Church, three models will be found:

- Traditional Church, re-shaped, opened up and user-friendly with worship which is vibrant and relevant for those attending.

- Fresh expressions, sometimes meeting on church premises and sometimes not; certainly not tied to Sunday for their worship. The result of 'pioneering ministries'.

- 'Ecclesial communities' ('emerged church'), transient, often counter-cultural and springing up through the Spirit, but requiring very special gifts of ministry.

What I am suggesting is not new. Indeed, the last model was being advanced in the 1960s and 70s, but suffered from a secularized theology. Then along came charismatic renewal, bringing effervescent spirituality but containing within itself the sectarian seeds of polarization and other-worldliness. Transformation requires a theological synthesis.

Cultures old and new

Our culture is very different from the 1960s and 70s. It is no longer optimistic. It is more diverse, plural and violent. We failed to seize opportunities then; will it be any different now when God's judgement is falling more heavily upon the Church?

If the Church in Britain is to be transformed there appears to be only two choices on offer at the moment. Either one joins a church with clear evangelical convictions and boundaries, demanding a heavy commitment to Christ, or one opts for places which provide 'holy space' but demand little of the worshipper. Traditional churches on the lookout for newcomers to run their existing programmes and organization will probably not survive, since faithfulness is in short supply. Theologically illiterate churches or churches attempting to hold their congregations by dumbing down worship or 'rebranding' their building or their product will similarly fail. This does not mean that conservative evangelical churches hold the key to the future. Old-fashioned biblical fundamentalism is on the way out in this country, even though it may be gaining ground in the US and other parts of the world.

Grace Davie points out that within our consumer culture the 'feel-good' factor is high on the list of people's needs. Evangelical churches with charismatic worship usually provide this 'feel-good' factor but so too does the tranquillity of a cathedral evensong or the mystery of an Orthodox liturgy. Today people want to *feel* something; an experience of the holy. The purely cerebral has little appeal.

On the edge of Pentecost, the Church faces a major challenge. Although many churches will be wiped out in the next 10 years, some will survive and thrive and therein lies the theological challenge. Their survival will be dependent in part on how accommodating they are of our consumer culture but also on their willingness to be suitably counter-cultural. Theological reflection is essential if churches are to cross the threshold of breakdown and reaggregation (page 11). They will need preacher's theology to feed them with the objectivity of the Word and save them from falling into the trap of fundamentalism. Second, they will need the critique of a proper charismatic theology to counter the subjectivity which so quickly evaporates into emotionalism. Third, they require a global theology to enlarge their vision and propel them into active engagement with issues of peace and justice for the marginalized and for the planet.

Ministry across frontiers

Gone are the days when one pattern of ministry fits all. It seems likely that church buildings will become more peripheral. An increasing number of ordained ministers will operate across frontiers as chaplains and priests for everyone. There are two reasons for this. First, there is no longer a correlation between the numerical growth of a congregation and the presence of an ordained minister; indeed, the entrenched attitudes of some local churches are the principal cause of clergy stress. Such congregations believe the minister's job is to bring back the halcyon days of full churches by using the same programme of activities which was on offer 30 or 40 years ago, regardless of demographic and cultural change. They prefer to travel, as some rail passengers do, with their backs to the future. Is God calling fewer persons into the traditional priesthood so as to break the dependency of the local church on its clergy and set the laity free?

Second, ordained and theologically trained persons are needed, like the apostle Paul, to operate cross-culturally. More opportunities for spiritual dialogue present themselves on such frontiers than within the local church. As a chaplain in Asda remarked, 'I have more conversations here about God on a Friday evening than I ever do in the local church on Sunday.'

Clergy old and new

So what of the local church? David Clark, in his book *Breaking the Mould of Christendom*, argues for a renewal of the diaconate whose primary role is to be a community educator through being an enabler and catalyst within the Church. The local church will then become a diaconal church serving the world. Leaving on one side his comments about the diaconate, he is certainly correct to insist that churches must become open communities of learning. The main purpose of this book is to encourage your church to be a theological community; a place where people become aware of the rich inheritance of Christ and know what it means to claim that inheritance for themselves and for others.

What of the ordained priests, presbyters and bishops? There will be fewer of them. They will be charismatic in the proper sense of the word, though not like Samson, the Rambo of the Old Testament who specialized in charismatic vandalism. He was undoubtedly handy with a donkey's jawbone but his final act brought the house down. The Church may occasionally need a few tough men and women to drive through programmes of change; however, leading the Church across the border-land of transformation requires a different type of minister. The ordained leader, marked by gentleness and humility, will not be afraid because she/he has already passed through a personal wilderness and knows how to live by faith and anticipate the surging release of Pentecost.

During the Communist occupation of Prague, Father Vlk was persecuted as a priest, thrown out of his parish and told he had to get a proper job. He became a window cleaner. One day he was working in one of Prague's busy streets and thought, 'No one knows I am a priest. No one cares about the gospel I preach.' Then a voice inside seemed to say, 'On the cross, God is present but hidden, and if Jesus could live and die in that way then so can you.' Several years later the Berlin Wall fell. Shortly afterwards he was made Archbishop.

Kairos and chronos

In my end-of-year address to the Methodist Conference I reflected on a text from Mark's Gospel: 'The time is fulfilled, and the kingdom of heaven is at hand; repent and believe in the good news' (Mk. 1.15).

There are two Greek words for 'time', *chronos* and *kairos*. The first word is 'clock-time' measured by chronometers, the second relates to that liminal moment when linear time and eternity are encapsulated in a single elective moment of opportunity. Unless an immediate response is made, God's *kairos* passes.

This sense of haste comes from a belief in the imminent advent of God's kingdom, anticipated in the arrival of successive waves of Spirit triggered by the first Pentecost. A *kairos* moment in mission marks the juxtaposition in time and space of God's renewing Spirit and our 'active word', for 'we are witnesses to these things, and so is the Holy Spirit, whom God has given to those who obey him' (Acts 5.32).

The Church hovers at a *'kairos* moment'. God is giving us a brief window of opportunity, possibly only five years, in which to turn ourselves around or, to be more accurate, 'to repent and believe'. To repent is another way of saying we must face reality and change decisively. To believe is another way of saying we must trust God and risk all. Whether we should picture this in terms of *Gone with the Wind* or *Back to the Future* I know not, but this I know: we must act quickly.

THEOLOGICAL EXPLORATION

- When did you last have a conversation about God with a person completely outside of the church? How did it go?

- On page 137 I gave a few indicators about churches which will or will not survive. What are the survival chances of your church?

- How do you respond to the suggestion that there will be fewer ordained persons looking after local churches and parishes and more operating in the community?

Question for the next chapter

How ready and equipped are you to cope with changes bigger than you have ever faced before?

12

Bones on a Bicycle

Chapter 1 began with a description of my induction at the Methodist Conference of June 2005. On 22 June 2006 at Edinburgh my term of office came to a close. One of my colleagues, the Revd Chris Blake, spoke of my ministry. Here is an edited version of what he said:

> Mr President, Tom. To describe in a few minutes what you have brought to the Methodist Church over the last 12 months is almost impossible. You have invited us to re-engage with theology, you have challenged us to find new ways of being church, you have enabled us in worship and in study to encounter the holy and living God – and you have taken more photographs of the Connexion than any President in living memory! However, a quick survey among my colleagues has indicated that what we will call your 'spontaneous' way of working has not been easy for everyone to adapt to.
>
> Perhaps, having been your Synod secretary for three years, I was prepared for your visit to the Cornwall District and was not too surprised by the way we started the Saturday in advance of the Study Day you were leading. We needed to leave the house at

9.45 a.m. At 9.15 you asked me to produce 100 copies of the handout you expected to use. At 9.30 when I came to you with the requested copies I was not surprised to hear you say: 'We're not doing that any more – we're doing something else' – but perhaps I was a little taken aback when you looked at the photocopied sheets in my hand as if you couldn't remember asking for them in the first place. Needless to say, the Study Day was brilliant and greatly valued by all who attended.

My experience was not unique. Another colleague said to me, 'Tom was an absolute nightmare to work with! Sermons prepared on the back of an envelope during the hymn before scared me witless. But God, to my considerable dismay, seemed to use it!'

Tom, you have given people permission to take risks and you have, often in worship, invited people to respond in a practical way to indicate their renewed commitment to the path of discipleship.

The books you have written have shown how your global travels have enriched and challenged your faith. Perhaps a new book will be needed to speak of your experiences during this year. You have encouraged us to keep on being theologians and you have done this by making it clear that you see yourself as still on a journey of discovery.

You have spoken of the Church being 'on the edge of Pentecost' and of the encouraging signs of the Spirit. Of course the challenges remain, but during your Presidential year you have, through your vision, through inviting us to keep on doing theology and through the call to be open to the movement of the Spirit, enabled us all to be better equipped to face those challenges.

New horizons

In the closing weeks of my Presidency I was reminded that retirement was just around the corner. We would be 'downsizing' in more ways than one, moving from a large four-bedroom house with study to a two-bedroom bungalow, leaving a job I enjoyed and working out what life had in store for us. Barbara Glasson, who accompanied us to the Irish Conference, after several conversations with Christine, wrote the following poem and presented it to me at breakfast:

> On the platform you've sat like a resident.
> As retirement comes close you feel hesitant.
> Now, go where you feel
> Relax and freewheel
> Disembark from the office of President.
>
> But now there's a spoke in the plan.
> For Chris wants to claim back her man
> Put romance in your eyes
> And make you downsize
> No more sermon prep in the can.
>
> You may not have manse or great pay
> But as you pedal down to the bay
> Rejoice you're not saddled
> With complaints tired and addled
> There is scope for this cleric to play.

A pre-breakfast limber or hike
Just one sausage less than you'd like
An Adonis you'll feel and
Then off to New Zealand
A tall bag of bones on a bike.

It not only made me smile but has largely come true, apart from the 'free-wheeling' bit. To celebrate 40 years of marriage, the enrichment of our lives through our family, our retirement and the blessings of the Presidential year we decided to spoil ourselves with a trip to New Zealand. Although I led Bible studies at the Methodist Conference in Rotorua it was mainly a time of play. In that beautiful country, through conversations about the melting ice of Antarctica, the rising sea levels around the Pacific Islands and the hole in the ozone layer, we became more aware of the effects of carbon emissions and climate change. These issues sharpened up my belief that the planet itself is poised on a *kairos* threshold.

Humanity: a planetary disease?

It has been calculated that if everyone in the world were to consume natural resources and generate carbon dioxide at the rate we do in the UK we would need three planets to support us.

In November 2005 I attended a debate at the European Parliament in Strasbourg. Speaker after speaker reminded us that the greatest threat facing humankind does not come from the terrorist but from climate change. On 1 January 2007 the Pope said, 'Humanity, if it truly desires peace, must be increasingly conscious of the links between natural ecology and human ecology.'

The scientist and environmentalist James Lovelock has introduced us to the idea of Gaia. Gaia is the thin spherical shell of land and water between the incandescent interior of the Earth and the upper atmosphere surrounding it. Gaia regulates the climate and chemistry of the planet to support life. At one level we can think of Gaia as a mechanistic climate control system like the one in your car, but Lovelock goes further. He gives it purpose and identity like the goddess from whom the name is taken. In his popular book, *The Revenge of Gaia*, he dares to suggest that if we fail to take care of the earth, the earth will surely take care of itself by wiping us out, since we have become a planetary disease.[1]

If so, Thomas Hardy may be right after all in thinking of God as pitiless and indifferent:

> Let me enjoy the earth no less
> > Because the all-enacting might
> That fashioned forth its loveliness
> > Had other aims than my delight.
> And some day hence, towards Paradise
> > And all its blest – if such there be –
> I will lift glad, afar off eyes,
> > Though it contain no place for me.[2]

Some theological responses

Thomas Hardy's belief in blind fate is one possible response. If furious religion spawns violence and terror within countries and across continents you may, like Richard Dawkins, want nothing to do with religion.

I want to offer you a hopeful response to the future. This is one of my purposes in writing. The resignation of Hardy and the anger of Dawkins will not help you.

Christianity will! God's creative Spirit is already at work, not only in your own lives and those of your friends and neighbours, but in the planet itself. Mark Wallace writes:

> The Spirit is the green face of God, the intercessory force for peace and solidarity in a world saturated with sacrificial violence, the power of renewal within creation as the creation groans in travail and waits with eager longing for environmental justice.[3]

God has created us in his own image because he wants to share his glory with us. We are called to be partners and co-creators in an 'ecological mission'. God graciously gives us 'dominion'. The word 'dominion' has nothing to do with exploitation but rather of stewardship. Ours is a representative 'priestly' role for all the inhabitants of the planet. In the poetry of George Herbert:

> Of all the creatures both in sea and land
> Only to Man thou has made known thy ways
> And put the pen alone into his hand
> And made him secretary of thy praise.
> Man is the world's high priest: he doth
>   present
> The sacrifice for all . . .[4]

In the Sistine Chapel in Rome there are two visions of the future. Over the altar is Michelangelo's apocalyptic picture of the last judgement. On the ceiling are nine great panels portraying the opening chapters of the Genesis story from the creator God to the drunkenness of Noah. It was an illuminating discovery when I learnt that Michelangelo Buonarroti did not begin by painting God and moving on through the stages of creation to the deluge. He instead started with Noah's drunkenness and worked backwards. His was not a story of a fall downwards but of a fall upwards into God. Humankind is being invited to come of age as full grown sons and daughters of God.

In New Zealand Christine and I were able to fulfil a lifelong ambition to go whale watching, far out beyond the continental shelf bordering Kaikoura on the East coast of the South Island. We waited for a long time, and when I saw my first sperm whale surface, spurting jets of water and air, I was awestruck. Neither of us knew how long a whale basks on the surface, vulnerable and exposed. I found tears running down my face as we drew closer to this wonderful creature. These are our distant cousins from the deep. They care for their young, talk with each other and may somehow enshrine within themselves the self-consciousness of the planet. Do they reflect the divine image more than we human beings who hunt and kill them to extinction? For some 10 minutes he lay breathing before heaving his great body over to plunge into the depth, waving us a fond farewell with his great fluke. This was one of those illuminating 'numinous' moments when a profound personal interaction took place (page 17).

Pierre Teilhard de Chardin once wrote about creation becoming aware of itself through our gaze. We humans are the mirror for Gaia. I now understood for the first time that we not only live in the planet but also the planet lives in us. It is not that God is in all things but that all things are in God. This is immanent transcendence. Not only is the planet changing, we too are being transformed and brought by God to new liminal edges of our existence. Although shaped from the earth and a little lower than the angels, in Christ we have the potential to become true partners with God and guardians of the planet. 'Beloved, we are God's children now; what we will be has not yet been revealed. What we do know is this: when he is revealed, we will be like him, for we will see him as he is' (1 John 3.2). An inheritance beyond our wildest dreams awaits us.

For each of us, as we grow and develop, there are critical *kairos* moments when we stand on the edge of new possibilities. We need to recognize these occasions when they come, bring them to God and respond courageously. This is not easy, for these moments contain within themselves death and resurrection, brokenness and break-out. I have argued that the Church and the planet are grappling with a *kairos* moment. Christians in Britain stand on the edge of Pentecost as the Spirit seeks to reshape the Church into the vibrant vehicle of God's tomorrow.

The great mystery

In Chapter 4 I produced two creeds, the first written 37 years ago, the next 18 years ago. Here is my latest statement about God, produced in 2004. I included it in my address to the ministers of the Methodist Conference:

> Those who have read *Into the Far Country* will realize I have abandoned the traditional metaphysical concepts of omnipotence, omniscience and omnipresence. The God I believe in can no longer be described in these terms or always given a masculine gender. The trinitarian God of grace is an

interactive, creative, imaginative, community God who suffers, undergoes change, experiences pain and exemplifies love. This God who is invincible has chosen to be vulnerable in order to embrace us. He invites us to work with him in the task of recreating the world. The Trinitarian God whose Word is at the heart of all things sends waves of Spirit rippling through the universe. God's presence in the world is therefore personal, dynamic and interactive, for we are not only called to discern his presence but to engage in a partnership with him in the world.

In Chapter 1 I quoted Avery Dulles. Although concerned with symbol and mystery his theology never breaks out of a systematic framework to take wings and fly like poetic theology. Moreover, while recognizing the diversity of theology he still assumes this diversity can be adequately encapsulated by ecumenical theology. His theology exists to serve the Church. For me, theology exists to praise God. By its very nature theology seeks to be beautiful. It will always be provisional since God transcends theology. Scientists examining the world of sub-atomic particles speak of universes made up of 10 or 11 dimensions; something totally inconceivable for us who live in a four-dimensional world of time and space. Maybe the very notion of God as Trinity is itself too small!

While Dulles' exposition leads him to the university, my theological pilgrimage takes me to a local Christian community attempting to hear what the Spirit is saying, where every member wishes to participate in a downloading of their corporate millionaire inheritance. Rather than choosing Avery Dulles as my model theologian I prefer another Roman Catholic, Pablo Richard from Chile. 'In Europe,' he says, 'when you write you have a library of books behind you. When we write we have the people behind us.' Before he puts pen to paper he gives innumerable biblical workshops with local community leaders and listens to what they say. He then writes his book and follows it with more workshops, this time to communicate and check out his ideas. To some extent I have done this with my previous book, *Beyond the Box*. Much of this book is the grateful product of the reflections, conversation and stories of people I have met on the way. I want this book to be from the people and for the people.

The final threshold

Congratulations! You have faithfully travelled with me to this parting of the ways. How are you shaping up as a theologian? What has God been saying to you as you have traced your own life story through mine? Are you ready for the journey ahead? The stories and reflections of this book are preparing you for the final frontier; the transition from this world to the next through death.

Why do we link ageing and bodily deterioration with the advent of death rather than life? Just as we still feel young when we are old, maybe we are already old while we are young. Didn't Wordsworth say 'the Child is father of the Man'?[5] If in Christ the fall of Adam has been reversed then living is about getting younger rather than older. God is calling us to enter a garden of delights, not Eden or a lost paradise but a resurrection garden of hope (Jn 20.11–18). Mary met

151

Jesus there. He is going on another journey but Mary tries to hold him back. Jesus has therefore to point her to a new future. When we shake off our accumulated possessions and let go of everything which clutters the mind and heart, we start to view the world with wonder and wisdom. Transformation takes place through downsizing in the presence of God.

'Just as our mothers, when we were small, helped us to undress at night, to take off our clothes at the end of the day, so Christ begins to divest us of our ageing and ailing bodies.'[6] A millionaire inheritance awaits us. The first instalment of the Spirit is already here for the asking. Our full inheritance lies just across the border.

My final words are for you, Ben and Sam. You may recall that as a teenager I read St Augustine's *Confessions*. I included a passage on page 26. Here is another just for you:

> Late have I loved thee, thou art Beauty itself, ancient of days yet ever new. Too late have I loved thee! . . . Thou wert with me but I was not with Thee . . . Thou hast called and shouted and broken through my deafness; Thou hast touched me, and I burned for thy peace. When I shall hold thee fast with my whole self I shall nowhere have sorrow or stress, and my life shall be wholly alive, being wholly filled with thee.[7]

THEOLOGICAL EXPLORATION

- How important for you is the issue of climate change?

- How do you now picture God? You may want to look again at the creed or poem you produced in an earlier session.

- What message do you want to pass on to any grandchildren you may have?

Appendix 1 – Other Books

The following are a list of some of the significant and less technical books in the text and a few others of possible interest for the reader.

Martyn Atkins, *Resourcing Renewal: Shaping Churches for the emerging future*, Peterborough: Inspire, 2007.

Karl Barth, *The Word of God and the Word of Man*, New York: Harper & Row, 1957.

Karl Barth, *Church Dogmatics*, Edinburgh: T & T Clark, (many volumes). For an introduction and application for today I suggest William S. Johnson, *The Mystery of God, Karl Barth and the Postmodern Foundations of Theology*, Louisville: Westminster John Knox Press, 1997

Dietrich Bonhoeffer, *The Cost of Discipleship*, London: SCM Press, 1959.

Dietrich Bonhoeffer, *Letters and Papers from Prison*, London: Collins Fontana, 1960.

Callum Brown, *The Death of Christian Britain*, London and New York: Routledge, 2001.

Emil Brunner, *Our Faith*, London: SCM Press, 1962.

John Calvin, *Institutes of the Christian Religion*, The Library of Christian Classics Vol. XX, London: SCM Press, 1961.

L. William Countryman, *Living on the Border of the Holy*, Harrisburg: Morehouse Publishing, 1999.

David Clark, *Breaking the Mould of Christendom*, Peterborough: Epworth, 2005.

Kenneth Cracknell, *Towards a New Relationship*, London: Epworth Press, 1986.

Fred Craddock, *Overhearing the Gospel*, Nashville: Abingdon Press, 1978.

Steven Croft (ed.), *The Future of the Parish System; Shaping the Church of England for the 21st Century*, London: Church House Publishing, 2006.

Don Cupitt, *After God*, London: Weidenfeld & Nicholson, 1997.

Richard Dawkins, *The God Delusion*, London: Bantam, 2006.

C.H. Dodd, *Apostolic Preaching and its Developments*, London: Hodder and Stoughton, 1966.

Avery Dulles, *The Craft of Theology: From Symbol to System*, New York: Crossroad, 1992.

Duncan Forester, *Apocalypse Now, Reflections on faith in a time of terror*, Aldershot: Ashgate Publishing, 2005.

P.T. Forsyth, *Positive Preaching and the Modern Mind*, London: Independent Press, 1964.

Rosino Gibellini, *The Liberation Theology Debate*, London: SCM Press, 1987.

E. Graham, H. Walton, F. Ward, *Theological Reflection: Methods*, London: SCM Press, 2005.

Mary Grey, *The Wisdom of Fools*, London: SPCK, 1959.

Oliver James, *Affluenza*, London: Vermilion, 2006.

Philip Jenkins, *The Next Christendom*, New York: Oxford University Press, 2002.

Chalmers Johnson, *Blowback: The costs and consequences of American Empire*, New York: Time Warner Paperback, 2002.

Steven J. Land, *Pentecostal Spirituality*, Sheffield Academic Press, London: Continuum imprint, 2003.

Kenneth Leech, *Struggle in Babylon*, London: Sheldon Press, 1988.

C.S. Lewis, *The Four Loves*, London: Fontana, 1963.

James Lovelock, *The Revenge of Gaia*, London: Penguin Books, 2006.

Thomas Merton, *New Seeds of Contemplation*, Norfolk, CT: New Directions, 1962.

Jurgen Moltmann, *The Spirit of Life*, London: SCM Press, 1992.

Heribert Muhlen, *A Charismatic Theology*, London; Burns & Oates, 1978.

Rudolph Otto, *The Idea of the Holy*, London: Oxford University Press, 1923.

Michael Polanyi, *Personal Knowledge*, London: Routledge & Kegan Paul, 1962.

John A.T. Robinson, *Honest to God*, London: SCM Press, 1963.

Alan Roxburgh, *The Missionary Congregation, Leadership and Liminality*, Pennsylvania: Trinity Press, 1997.

Ray Simpson, in *Church of the Isles*, Suffolk: Kevin Mayhew, 2003.

Tom Stuckey, *Into the Far Country*, Peterborough: Epworth, 2003.

Tom Stuckey, *Beyond the Box*, Peterborough: Inspire, 2005.

Paul Tillich, *The Shaking of the Foundations*, Harmondsworth: Penguin, 1962.

Paul Tillich, *Systematic Theology Volumes 1, 2, 3*, University of Chicago Press, 1973, 1975, 1976.

Mark Wallace, *Fragments of the Spirit: Nature, Violence and the Renewal of Creation*, New York: Continuum International Publishing, 1997.

Vernon White, *Identity*, London: SCM Press, 2002.

Reports

Mission-shaped Church, London: Church House Publishing, 2004.

Changing church for a changing world, Fresh ways of being church in a Methodist context, London: Trustees for Methodist Church Purposes, 2007.

Notes

Chapter 1: Who Wants to be a Millionaire?

1. Leonard Cohen, 'Stranger Music', *Selected Poems and Songs*, London: Jonathan Cape, 1993.
2. Avery Dulles, *The Craft of Theology: From Symbol to System*, New York: Crossroad, 1992, p. 17.
3. Victor Turner, in Alan Roxburgh, *The Missionary Congregation, Leadership and Liminality*, Pennsylvania: Trinity Press, 1997.

Chapter 2: Break Out

1. E. Graham, H. Walton, F. Ward, *Theological Reflection: Methods*, London: SCM Press, 2005.
2. Paul Tillich, *The Shaking of the Foundations*, Harmondsworth: Penguin, 1962, p. 107.

Chapter 3: God is Dangerous

1. Book III, Dom Roger Hudleston (ed.), *The Confessions of St Augustine*, London: Collins, Fontana Books, 1957, p. 70.
2. Emil Brunner, *Our Faith*, London: SCM Press, 1962, p. 14.
3. *Methodist Recorder*, 13 October 2005.
4. L.William Countryman, *Living on the Border of the Holy*, Harrisburg: Morehouse Publishing, 1999, p. 186.
5. Emil Brunner, *Our Faith*, p. 17.
6. Karl Barth, *The Word of God and the Word of Man*, New York: Harper & Row, 1957, pp. 29f.
7. John Calvin, *Institutes of the Christian Religion* 1.5.12 (The Library of Christian Classics Vol. XX), London: SCM Press, 1961, p. 65.

Chapter 4: Cooking the Books

1. Francis Young and Kenneth Wilson, *Focus on God*, London: Epworth Press, 1986, p. 38.
2. E. Graham, H. Walton, F. Ward, *Theological Reflection: Methods*, London: SCM Press, 2005, pp. 109f.
3. Karl Barth, *Church Dogmatics, Vol. IV, Part 1*, Edinburgh: T & T Clark, 1961, p. 170.
4. Karl Barth, quoted in Robert McAfee Brown's 'Introduction' in George Casalis, *Portrait of Barth*, 3.

Chapter 5: A Preacher's Theology

1. Karl Barth, *Church Dogmatic, Vol. I, Part 1*, Edinburgh: T & T Clark, 1963, pp. 101f.
2. C.H. Dodd, *Apostolic Preaching and its Developments*, London: Hodder and Stoughton, 1966.
3. P.T. Forsyth, *Positive Preaching and the Modern Mind*, London: Independent Press, 1964, pp. 61f.
4. Annie Dillard, *Teaching a Stone to Talk: Expeditions and Encounters*, London: Picador, 1984, pp. 40-41.
5. P.T. Forsyth, *Positive Preaching and the Modern* Mind, p. 55.
6. Walter Brueggemann, *Mandate to Difference*, London: Westminster John Knox Press, 2007, pp. 73f.

Chapter 6: A Charismatic Theology

1. Steven J. Land, *Pentecostal Spirituality*, Sheffield Academic Press, London: Continuum imprint, 2003, p. 43.
2. Heribert Muhlen, *A Charismatic Theology*, London: Burns & Oates, 1978.
3. Jürgen Moltmann, *The Spirit of Life*, London: SCM Press, 1992, pp. 181f.

Chapter 7: A Global Theology

1. Found in Rosino Gibellini, *The Liberation Theology Debate*, London: SCM Press, 1987, p. 4.
2. *Methodist Recorder*, 15 October 1987.
3. Tom Stuckey, *Into the Far Country*, Peterborough: Epworth, 2003, p. 80.
4. *Partners in Practice*, British Council of Churches 1987.

5. Graham, Walton, Ward, *Theological Reflection: Methods*, London: SCM Press, 2005, p. 96.

Chapter 8: Transitions and Transformation

1. Mary Grey, *The Wisdom of Fools*, London: SPCK, 1959.
2. Don Cupitt, *After God*, London: Weidenfeld & Nicholson, 1997, pp. 110f.
3. Thomas Merton, *New Seeds of Contemplation*, Norfolk, CT: New Directions, 1962, p. 297.
4. Tom Stuckey, *Beyond the Box*, Inspire, 2005, pp. 57f.

Chapter 9: Apocalypse Now

1. T.S. Eliot, 'Burnt Norton', *The Four Quartets*, London: Faber & Faber Ltd, 2001.
2. Chalmers Johnson, *Blowback: The costs and consequences of American Empire*, New York: Time Warner Paperback, 2002.
3. Nanette Stahl, *Law and Liminality in the Bible*, Sheffield Academic Press, 1995, pp. 76f.

Chapter 10: Pentecost

1. *Methodist Recorder*, 1 September 2005.
2. Martyn Atkins, *Resourcing Renewal: Shaping Churches for the emerging future*, Peterborough: Inspire, 2007, p. 59.
3. Thomas Merton, *No Man is an Island,* London: Burns & Oates, 1955, p. 209.
4. Oliver James, *Affluenza*, London: Vermilion, 2006.

Chapter 11: Churches Old and New

1. Graham Carter in the *Methodist Recorder*, 5 April 2007.
2. Figures quoted by Ray Simpson in *Church of the Isles*, Suffolk: Kevin Mayhew, 2003, p. 25.
3. Poem similarly quoted by Ray Simpson, p. 34.
4. Martin Percy, *Many rooms in my Father's house: The changing identity of the English parish church* in Steven Croft (ed.), *The Future of the Parish System: Shaping the Church of England for the 21ˢᵗ Century*, London: Church House Publishing, 2006, p. 12.

5. Grace Davie, *From obligation to consumption: Understanding the patterns of religion in Northern Europe*, in Steven Croft (ed.) *The Future of the Parish System*, p. 40.
6. John Hull, *Mission-shaped Church*, London: Church House Publishing, 2004.

Chapter 12: Bones on a Bicycle

1. James Lovelock, *The Revenge of Gaia*, Santa Barbara, CA: Allen Lane, 2006.
2. Thomas Hardy, 'Let me enjoy the earth no less', from *A Set of Country Songs* (1898).
3. Mark Wallace, *Fragments of the Spirit: Nature, Violence and the Renewal of Creation*, New York: Continuum International Publishing, 1997.
4. George Herbert, 'Providence', from *The Temple* (1683).
5. William Wordsworth, 'My heart leaps up' (1807).
6. Michael Walker, *The God of our Journey*, London: Marshal-Pickering, 1989, pp. 130ff.
7. Augustine, *Confessions*, Book X, xxvii.38.